CLASSIC LIVES

CAROLINE SILVER

CLASSIC LIVES

The Education of a Racehorse

HARCOURT BRACE JOVANOVICH, INC.
NEW YORK

Library of Congress Cataloging in Publication Data

Silver, Caroline, 1938-
Classic lives.

1. Race horses—Great Britain. 2. Horse-training.
3. Epsom Derby. 4. Thoroughbred horse. I. Title.
SF351.S55   1973   636.1   73-6729
ISBN 0-15-118130-6

First American edition

B C D E

In memory of Michael Ryan
who helped me so much

CONTENTS

ILLUSTRATIONS

Between pages 128 and 129

ACKNOWLEDGMENTS

I OWE this book to the kindness and patience of a great many people. I would like particularly to thank the following:

The Earl of Derby and Mr Bernard van Cutsem, without whose consent and co-operation there would have been no book;

At Lavington Stud: Colonel Sydney Kennedy, Mr Wally Claydon;

At Woodlands Stud: Colonel Adrian Scrope, Mr Michael Ryan, Mr Dick Nicholls;

At Knowsley: Mr Colin Dive;

At Calverstown House Stud: Mr and Mrs Peter McCall, Mr Peter Kelly;

At Prospect Stud: Dr John Burkhardt;

At Stanley House Stables: Messrs Stanley Warren, Jack Banks, Arthur Bell, Bob Bland, Ray Coppola, George Douglas, Tony Leaman, Matty McCormack, Michael Ryan, Mrs Maureen Foley.

These people allowed me to watch and to participate in all the aspects of British and Irish stud, stable and racing life that are described in the book. Without their generous co-operation, I could not possibly have reconstructed the lives of the horses. Colin Dive, Mick Ryan Sr, and Stan Warren were outstandingly helpful.

Mr Derrick and Mr Henry Candy let me ride their horses for a year, and taught me much about racing at first hand. Mr

Willie Carson, who in 1971 rode 792 races (over 160 more than any other jockey), had total recall of an astonishing 55 of the 59 races about which I asked him. Mr Bill Curling and Mr G. Warnecke of Weatherbys got me passes to stables and racecourses and gave great help with the classic entries of 1968. Mr A. W. Gentry of the British Museum (Natural History) gave me the information about Eclipse which appears on page 123. Mr David Hedges, Director, International Racing Bureau, told me about American and French racing. Miss Dorothy Laird of the Racing Information Bureau was tirelessly helpful and patient, as was Mr Denis Lyonson, private secretary to Lord Derby. Mr Russ Maddock remembered Mountain Call with clarity and humour. Mr Frank Osgood, Manager and Secretary of Newbury Racecourse, told me what happens to a racecourse when the public isn't there. Jim Peden Air Transport flew me to Ireland and back with a cargo of horses. Mr and Mrs David Ringer filled me in with Newmarket stories and atmosphere.

Prince Richard of Gloucester, my parents Mr and Mrs Philip Green, and Mr Richard Berens generously gave me a place to write when I had none.

Roger Mortimer's excellent *Encyclopaedia of Flat Racing*, and *Your Horse, A Veterinary Book*, published by the *Sporting Life*, provided much information. The *Sporting Life* and the racing correspondents of *The Times* and the *Daily Telegraph* gave me quotes. Roddy Maude-Roxby, Nathan Silver, Bill Steele and Sue Wood took most of the photographs.

Mr Barrett Best, Henry Candy, Mr and Mrs Tony Clayton, Colin Dive, Mick Ryan and Stan Warren read and corrected the manuscript. Mrs Janet Dawes typed it, twice. David Machin, Ed Barber and Mike Petty edited it.

There are others — such as the man who showed me how starting gates are operated, and the farmer in a Shropshire pub who first explained to me *why* old grass is sweeter — whose names I can no longer remember. To them, as to all the people listed above, I am deeply grateful.

Crooked Soley, Wiltshire   C.S.
Autumn 1972

FOREWORD

IN THE summer of 1967 a photographer suggested an unusual story to a London magazine. He wanted to do the pictorial biography of a runner in the Derby. His plan was to follow the horse's career from birth to three years old, the age at which the Derby is run, and to publish the story just before the race. He would therefore need to take photographs over a period of about three-and-a-half years. I was asked to supply the words. All we needed was to find a foal who would grow up to be a Derby runner.

In 1967 6,021 thoroughbred foals were born in Britain. In the same year 590 horses were named for the 1968 Derby at the initial stage of entry, the spring of their two-year-old year, although about forty per cent of these were from France or Ireland. When the time came around for the 1968 Derby only thirteen of the original 590 were still down to run.

The most prestigious races for flat horses in England are the five 'classics': the One Thousand Guineas, the Two Thousand Guineas, the Derby, the Oaks, and the St Leger. All are for three-year-olds only, and a victory in any one of them will ensure the winner's value at stud. But the greatest race of the lot is the Derby. The moment the winner goes past the post his value is assured at not less than £250,000. Most Derby winners are home-bred by owner-breeders who regard the British racing prize with little less than fanaticism.

The theory is, 'Breed the best to the best and hope for the best.' Many try it, but few succeed. Why?

A classically bred horse is one whose sire or dam has won one of the five classic races, and who can therefore expect to be suited to the Derby distance of one mile and a half. Of the six thousand or so thoroughbreds foaled each year in Britain only about a thousand are classically bred. The odds against choosing a 1968 Derby horse at birth were thus roughly 1000–13, or 75–1. That was the end of the magazine project.

I wondered why it should be so difficult to produce a classic runner. The cost of breeding and training a racehorse is high – stud fees to a classic sire vary from £500 to £10,000, and once the foal is born it will cost upwards of £1,000 a year to keep until the end of its racing career. Only about five per cent of all racehorses cover their costs, but, happily, owners are enthusiasts who do not try to economize. Handling does not seem to be the problem, either: most of these horses are magnificently cared for. It seemed that the risks must lie in the peculiarities, physical or mental, of the horses themselves. Or is it just luck?

I began to study half a dozen horses who were foaled in 1965. I wanted to find out a little about what could go wrong, or right, in their early lives. All but one were classically bred. The exception, a sprinter, interested me because of slight differences in his upbringing and character. To make any kind of comparison possible I needed horses who were bred by the same owner and trained by the same trainer; that is, horses whose chances at birth seemed to be equal. I was lucky enough to get, and am extremely grateful for, per-mission to follow horses owned by a man whose name must be the most famous in British racing and trained by one of the outstanding trainers in the country.

This book is about horses who belonged to the eighteenth Earl of Derby and who were trained by Bernard van Cutsem. It is a biography of half a dozen of them from birth to their classic season. While I hope it may show some of the risks involved in breeding and training, it does not offer any solutions.

EXTRACTS FROM STUD BOOK
RECORDS

Relic	War Relic	Man O'War	Fair Play	Hastings Fairy Gold
			Mahubah	Rock Sand Merry Token
		Friar's Carse	Friar Rock	Rock Sand Fairy Gold
			Problem	Superman Query
	Bridal Colors	Black Toney	Peter Pan	Commando Cinderella
			Belgravia	Ben Brush Bonnie Gal
		Vaila	Fariman	Gallinule Bellinzona
			Padilla	Macheath Padua
Sunsuit	Alycidon	Donatello II	Blenheim	Blandford Malva
			Delleana	Clarissimus Duccia di Buoninsegna
		Aurora	Hyperion	Gainsborough Selene
			Rose Red	Swynford Marchetta
	Herringbone	King Salmon	Salmon-Trout	The Tetrarch Salamandra
			Malva	Charles O'Malley Wild Arum
		Schiaparelli	Schiavoni	Swynford Serenissima
			Aileen	Nimbus Yveline

CHESTNUT COLT / GAMECOURT / FOALED IN 1965					
Match III	Tantieme	Deux Pour Cent	Deiri	Aethelstan / Desra
			Dix Pour Cent	Feridoon / La Chansonnière
		Terka	Indus	Alcantara II / Himalaya
			La Furka	Blandford / Brenta
	Relance III	Relic	War Relic	Man O'War / Friar's Carse
			Bridal Colors	Black Toney / Vaila
		Polaire	Le Volcan	Tourbillon / Eroica
			Stella Polaris	Papyrus / Crepuscule
Bluecourt	Court Martial	Fair Trial	Fairway	Phalaris / Scapa Flow
			Lady Juror	Son-in-Law / Lady Josephine
		Instantaneous	Hurry On	Marcovil / Tout Suite
			Picture	Gainsborough / Plymstock
	Alcyone	Alycidon	Donatello II	Blenheim / Delleana
			Aurora	Hyperion / Rose Red
		Manetta	Nearco	Pharos / Nogara
			Wafer	Sansovino / Waffles

CHESTNUT FILLY	INDOLENT	FOALED IN 1965			
		Tyrone	Tornado	Tourbillon	Ksar	Brûleur Kizil Kourgan
					Durban	Durbar Banshee
				Roseola	Swynford	John O'Gaunt Canterbury Pilgrim
					Roseway	Stornoway Rose of Ayrshire
			Statira	Static	Aethelstan	Teddy Dédicace
					Fanatic	Durbar Fanager
				Fantastic	Teddy	Ajax Rondeau
					Listen In	Rabelais Lisette IX
		Lazybones	Never Say Die	Nasrullah	Nearco	Pharos Nogara
					Mumtaz Begum	Blenheim Mumtaz Mahal
				Singing Grass	War Admiral	Man O'War Brushup
					Boreale	Vatout Galaday II
			Wake Up!	Persian Gulf	Bahram	Blandford Friar's Daughter
					Double Life	Bachelor's Double Saint Joan
				Arousal	Fairway	Phalaris Scapa Flow
					Aurora	Hyperion Rose Red

LAUREATE BAY COLT FOALED IN 1965	Aureole	Hyperion	Gainsborough	Bayardo	Bay Ronald Galicia
				Rosedrop	St Frusquin Rosaline
			Selene	Chaucer	St Simon Canterbury Pilgrim
				Serenissima	Minoru Gondolette
		Angelola	Donatello II	Blenheim	Blandford Malva
				Delleana	Clarissimus Duccia di Buoninsegna
			Feola	Friar Marcus	Cicero Prim Nun
				Aloe	Son-in-Law Alope
	Sundry	Nearco	Pharos	Phalaris	Polymelus Bromus
				Scapa Flow	Chaucer Anchora
			Nogara	Havresac II	Rabelais Hors Concours
				Catnip	Spearmint Sibola
		Sundae	Hyperion	Gainsborough	Bayardo Rosedrop
				Selene	Chaucer Serenissima
			Bachelor's Fare	Tredennis	Kendal St Marguerite
				Lady Bawn	Le Noir Milady

CHESTNUT COLT — MOUNTAIN CALL — FOALED IN 1965					
Whistler	Panorama	Sir Cosmo	The Boss	Orby Southern Cross II
			Ayn Hali	Desmond Lalla Rookh
		Happy Climax	Happy Warrior	Sundridge Sweet Lassie
			Clio	Dark Ronald Mall
	Farthing Damages	Fair Trial	Fairway	Phalaris Scapa Flow
			Lady Juror	Son-in-Law Lady Josephine
		Futility	Solario	Gainsborough Sun Worship
			Hasty Love	Hurry On Love-oil
Cloudy Walk	Nimbus	Nearco	Pharos	Phalaris Scapa Flow
			Nogara	Havresac II Catnip
		Kong	Baytown	Achtoi Princess Herodias
			Clang	Hainault Vibration
	Sun Lane	Hyperion	Gainsborough	Bayardo Rosedrop
			Selene	Chaucer Serenissima
		Celestial Way	Fairway	Phalaris Scapa Flow
			Princess Sublime	King William Sublime

FOALED IN 1965 / RAINHILL / CHESTNUT COLT	Mossborough	Nearco	Pharos	Phalaris	Polymelus / Bromus
				Scapa Flow	Chaucer / Anchora
			Nogara	Havresac II	Rabelais / Hors Concours
				Catnip	Spearmint / Sibola
		All Moonshine	Bobsleigh	Gainsborough	Bayardo / Rosedrop
				Toboggan	Hurry On / Glacier
			Selene	Chaucer	St Simon / Canterbury Pilgrim
				Serenissima	Minoru / Gondolette
	Samanda	Alycidon	Donatello II	Blenheim	Blandford / Malva
				Delleana	Clarissimus / Duccia di Buoninsegna
			Aurora	Hyperion	Gainsborough / Selene
				Rose Red	Swynford / Marchetta
		Gradisca	Goya II	Tourbillon	Ksar / Durban
				Zariba	Sardanapale / St Lucre
			Phebe	Pharos	Phalaris / Scapa Flow
				La Grelée	Helicon / Grignous

FOALED IN 1965 / **SHE WOLF** / **BAY FILLY**	Hugh Lupus	Djebel	Tourbillon	Ksar	Brûleur / Kizil Kourgan
				Durban	Durbar / Banshee
			Loika	Gay Crusader	Bayardo / Gay Laura
				Coeur à Coeur	Teddy / Ballantrae
		Sakountala	Goya II	Tourbillon	Ksar / Durban
				Zariba	Sardanapale / St Lucre
			Samos	Brûleur	Chouberski / Basse Terre
				Samya	Nimbus / Sapience
	Dilettante	Dante	Nearco	Pharos	Phalaris / Scapa Flow
				Nogara	Havresac II / Catnip
			Rosy Legend	Dark Legend	Dark Ronald / Golden Legend
				Rosy Cheeks	Saint Just / Purity
		Herringbone	King Salmon	Salmon-Trout	The Tretrarch / Salamandra
				Malva	Charles O'Malley / Wild Arum
			Schiaparelli	Schiavoni	Swynford / Serenissima
				Aileen	Nimbus / Yveline

1965

Winter

WEDNESDAY, February 3rd, was dry and cold. A pale afternoon sun glinted off patches of snow that hung around, frost-hard, in hollows, and turned the tall dead grasses gold. The bare oaks, elms, and horse-chestnuts on Lavington Stud in Sussex became a warmer brown in the thin yellow light, the creosoted three-rail wood fencing and the boarded wind-breaks in the paddock corners showed up black and hard. In the paddocks the pregnant thoroughbred mares, their heavy winter coats fluffed up against the cold, began to graze their way slowly towards the paddock gates where they would wait to be taken in for the night.

Mares due to foal were pastured in the two paddocks nearest to the foaling yard, so that they could easily be watched and brought in if necessary. Mares seldom foal during the day, and the one occupant of the foaling paddocks (most thoroughbred foals are born later in the spring) had given no cause for anxiety, though her udder had been 'bagged up' full of milk for the past two days and she had just 'waxed' – a thickish secretion had oozed from each milk canal and dried into wax-like blobs on her teats upon contact with the air. These were signs that birth could be expected during the next forty-eight hours, and might easily happen that night. Wally Claydon, the stud groom, noticed the waxing when he came to fetch the mare in for the night. He had been gently handling her udder every day for the past

week, partly to be sure he noticed when she first began to bag up
and partly because she was a maiden mare and needed to get
used to having her ticklish udder handled before her foal made
its first clumsy attempts at sucking. Claydon admired the mare
very much. She was a big chestnut five-year-old, exceptionally
good-looking, with very wide-set eyes and a will of her own.
Her name was Sunsuit, and she belonged to the Earl of
Derby. She had arrived at Lavington twenty-three days
before – early enough to allow her to develop the local im-
munities to disease that her new-born foal would need.
Later, when the foal had been born, she would visit the
resident stallion, Relko. Now she waited at the gate,
impatient to be brought in, and Claydon had some
trouble shifting her out of the way so that he could get the gate
open.

She led in easily enough, pulling on the lead rope in her
eagerness to get to her evening feed, but when they arrived
in the stable yard mare and groom had a difference of opinion;
Sunsuit wanted to go to her usual wooden loosebox and
Claydon wanted her in a brick foaling box for the night. The
groom was firm, and led Sunsuit into the clean, deep wheat
straw, showing her the feed that waited in the manger in the
corner. He saw that she had hay and clean water, brushed off
the worst of the mud that she had picked up in the paddock,
ran his hand over her full udder with the wax on both teats,
and noted that the muscles around her tail looked hollow
and slack. When he pressed the usually firm skin of her
rump the muscles felt flaccid, so she would probably foal
that night. (This slackening of Sunsuit's pelvic muscles was
caused by the hormone *relaxin*, which softens the tension of
the strong pelvic ligaments to facilitate the passage of the

foetus through the pelvis. Slackening usually starts about twelve to eighteen hours before the foal is born.)

Before he closed the top of the double stable door to shut her in for the night, Claydon leaned for a moment on the lower half to look at the big handsome mare. He had grown fond of her during her three-week stay, and liked her independent but kindly nature. He was almost sure he would be called out of bed during the night to deliver her first foal; now that the foaling season was beginning again, he thought, he would be lucky to get two full nights in bed a week during the next three months. And then, just when he had got really attached to the mare and to the foal that he had delivered himself, the owners would come and take the two away and he would never see them again, except perhaps when they came up for auction. But possibly the mare would be sent back to Lavington another year, and maybe in two or three years' time he would go to the racetrack and look through his racecard and think, I foaled that. And that, too. Almost every year now Claydon decided it was his last season, but each spring's foaling caught him up again. He could not make the decision to retire.

He went off to see to his other horses before tea, and soon it was dark and the yard was quiet except for the rustle of straw and the soft crunching of the mares finishing their evening feeds. A new moon was setting. As the last man left the yard the sitting-up man, who was to keep watch over the mares during the night, settled himself in the sitting-up room between the two main foaling boxes. From there he could keep an eye on Sunsuit through the window in the dividing wall. Periodically during the evening he made the rounds of the mares. At ten o'clock he was joined by Claydon for a final inspection before the stud groom went to bed.

The night was clear and very cold. At ten minutes to three the sitting-up man heard Sunsuit making more noise with her straw than he had so far noticed. He put down his book and looked through the window into the lighted loosebox. The mare was pulling up her bed with a forefoot and there were dark patches of sweat on her chestnut neck. He telephoned Claydon immediately. Two minutes later the stud groom was with him, wearing trousers and a heavy sweater over his pyjamas. Together the men looked through the window; Sunsuit was feeding quietly, a light steam rising from her sweaty neck in the cold air. After ten minutes she began to walk restlessly around the box, then stopped with a sudden intake of breath and turned her head to look at her nearside flank. She switched her tail, walked to her pile of hay in the corner of the box, and settled down to eat. For the next half hour or so nothing happened; Sunsuit ate calmly, the sweat dried on her neck, and Claydon and the sitting-up man talked quietly in front of the warm stove; then, at almost four o'clock, the mare became more obviously uneasy, pawing up her bed again, and half crouching as if about to lie down. She looked mildly worried; her eyes were wider open than before and her nostrils were distended. Her ears flicked nervously around, and a fresh light sweat broke out on her coat. Then the contraction passed and she settled down once more, but the two watchers knew they had not long to wait.

At four twenty-five Sunsuit got down in her straw, rolled over on her side, and groaned a couple of times. Then she got up, sweating heavily. Claydon rolled up his sleeves, washed his hands and arms carefully in disinfected water in the sitting-up room sink, and slipped quietly into the foaling box. He spoke soothingly to the mare. She allowed him to swab out her vagina and rectum and the surrounding areas with a solution of antiseptic, and to put a clean tail bandage on her to keep stray hairs out of the way of the foaling.

At four thirty Sunsuit's water bag slipped out and hung behind her and one of the foal's forelegs stuck out too, encased in thick white membrane. She got down again, rolling over a little to try and ease the pain. Claydon's quiet voice, the grunts of the labouring mare, and the rustle of flattened straw seemed loud in the still stable yard. Claydon put on a pair of disinfected rubber gloves and reached into the mare's vagina to see if the foal was in the correct position (if not, he would try to straighten it out before damage was done to the mare). He felt the other foreleg, straightened out a few inches behind the first, and then the head, pointed neatly on top of the legs like a diver. Satisfied then that the foal's shoulders would pass on a slant through the narrow pelvic area, avoiding damage to the mare, and that its muzzle would not be stuck against the roof of her vagina, he withdrew his arm to let the mare get on with it by herself.

Sunsuit put a lot into her labour, bearing down hard and regularly. After seven minutes the foal slipped easily out and lay in the clean straw, part of its hind legs still resting in the birth canal of the mare. The watching men stayed very quiet while the blood that was left in the placenta flowed through the connecting umbilical cord into the foal. Then, its muzzle and forelegs sticking out of the amniotic sac, the foal gave a little gasp in the cold air and began to breathe. Claydon turned on the warm-air blower in the box, felt the umbilical cord to make sure that the blood had stopped flowing, and then quickly stripped the foal of its covering membrane. It lay in the straw, soaking wet with fluid; a dark bay filly foal by Relic out of Sunsuit, later to be named Bikini.

Ten minutes after birth Bikini made struggling motions to get away from her dam, and in doing so she hooked her foreleg over the now useless umbilical cord and broke it. Claydon sprayed the broken end of the cord with disinfectant; then together the men lifted her to a position by Sunsuit's head where the mare, still lying down, began to lick her new-born foal dry. Bikini made an effort to get up, struggling against the newness of gravity (the weight of the foetal foal is cushioned by the fluids in the uterus and by its mother's intestines), of breathing, of a temperature drop of some 50 degrees from her warm foetal life, and of her long and un-manageable limbs, which are born almost adult-length on a foal's tiny body. Encouraged by licks from Sunsuit, which also stimulated her circulation, Bikini thrashed about in the straw trying to get her legs under her. After each effort she took a rest to get her strength back.

At five eleven Sunsuit got up with her afterbirth hanging down, leaving a mess of bloody straw beneath her. The men pulled Bikini by her forelegs onto clean straw in a corner and pitchforked out the birthed-in straw, replacing it with a very thick, clean bed; then they tied up the placenta in a bundle with disinfected string to prevent Sunsuit from stepping on it or kicking at it. It would come away later of its own weight, but it was important to keep it intact for subsequent examina-tion to see that it was all there, since a partly-retained placenta usually leads to infection. Meanwhile Bikini's crablike hops began to show results—at five nineteen, being a big, strong foal, she scrambled to her feet but fell down again im-mediately. Sunsuit knuckered encouragement to her daughter, though she was soon distracted by the aches of her own stomach as the tired muscles contracted. She got down in the straw to rest, rolling a little to ease the hurting. These pains, which are like a sore colic, can be relieved by an injection or, if the pains are excessive, by a foaling draught containing opium which is poured down the mare's throat. If the pain is intense a mare may roll wildly in an effort to relieve it and can become so preoccupied with her agony that she accidentally rolls on her foal. To avoid any danger of that, Claydon kept Bikini clear until Sunsuit's contractions stopped. When the pain eased, Sunsuit got up and her afterbirth came away. She lay down again to rest, and Claydon carried the afterbirth away in a bucket to keep for the morning.

At five thirty-seven Bikini got up again and fell down; at five forty she was on her feet, wobbling, and Sunsuit got up too, stretched, smelled her foal, and began to eat a warm bran mash with oats in it. Bikini lost her balance again, but regained it and in ten minutes was poking at the side of her dam to find a teat. She had no notion of where it could be; she searched around the mare's underbelly and tail, saliva running in a fine slobber down her lips, and then licked her mother's hind leg. Sunsuit shifted a little to get the foal's head nearer to the milk, then swung her nose out of the manger and pushed Bikini up from behind, towards the udder. Bikini let out a small knucker and went on feeling around, this time more or less in the right area. She found the teat at six nine and began to suck.

The whole operation from birth to Bikini's first feed had taken an hour and a half. Claydon felt he could now safely leave the mother and child by themselves. After nearly three and a half hours of close attention, with some heavy labour thrown in, he was tired; yet outside it would soon be morning and time for another day's work. He went home to catch a few minutes' sleep before the new day began.

II

The dawn came clear and cold. Sunrise at twenty to eight sparkled on a white frost in the paddocks, and patches of steamy breath rose from the men busy in the stable yard with the morning feeds. Claydon came from breakfast to look with pride at Sunsuit and her fine foal. He was joined by Colonel Sydney Kennedy, the stud manager, who had already telegrammed the good news to Lord Derby.

When the morning routine of feeding, examining, and getting the mares out to the paddocks had been done with, Claydon took Sunsuit's afterbirth from its bucket and carefully laid it out on the ground. It was shaped like pyjama trousers — open at the waist where Bikini's body had been pushed through, with legs closed at the stretched-out ends where her hind legs had pushed. It was all there. The veterinary surgeon arrived and approved it, and then gave Sunsuit a routine examination. Her vagina was stretched and loose from the passage of the big foal, so he put a couple of stitches in it to guard against wind-sucking from behind which might draw in infection.

Later in the day the mare and foal were moved back to Sunsuit's regular loosebox. Bikini was too babyish to have full control over her gangly hundred-pound body, so two men half-carried her along behind her mother.

On the third day after foaling, Sunsuit was taken alone to a small boarded paddock and freed for ten minutes' exercise.

She galloped about, bucking and kicking and calling for her foal, but the high boards prevented her from jumping out. The exercise worked the top off her energy before Bikini was let loose with her.

While the mare was stretching her legs, Bikini was fitted with a small foal headcollar. She fidgeted and worried and called out for her mother, paying little attention to her first piece of harness. When Sunsuit returned grooms led them both across the yard to a large covered school for exercise. Another man pushed Bikini from behind, so that she should learn to follow the pull on her headcollar. Indoor schooling is intended to teach the foal to follow the mare without risk of damage from a fall on hard ground, or of bewilderment from the mare's natural wish to go off at full gallop if turned loose into an open space. Padding along in the peat, Bikini got the hang of using her legs and was soon cantering along behind her dam.

The following day, after a short stretch alone for Sunsuit in the boarded paddock, the two were turned out in a nursery paddock together. On the morning of February 9th Bikini was given a routine anti-tetanus injection. The tetanus germ is very prevalent in cultivated soil and horse dung, but is harmless unless entering through a wound; young foals risk infection through the 'wound' of the broken umbilical cord. The day after the injection, Bikini and Sunsuit were put into a paddock with other mares who had foals of the same age. They were pastured in good company – Relko, an outstanding stallion insured for £400,000 and earning a stud fee of £3,000 from each of his forty-three mares a year, was bringing top-quality mares to Lavington for his services.

Relko, a French-bred horse, is the grandson of Bikini's sire,

Relic, who was bred in 1945 in America, where he won five races worth $72,300 and retired to stud in 1950. The following year Relic went to stud in France, where he stood for six years before coming to England in 1957. He now stands at the Longholes Stud, Newmarket, where Sunsuit visited him in 1964. Relic is a great stallion: his American offspring have won more than 150 races and $1,113,000 in prize money; his French offspring over 300 races and 2,000,000 francs; his English offspring over 170 races and £190,000. He isn't finished yet.

One of Relic's most famous children is the great French mare, Relance III, who has produced winners of most of the French classics, the English Derby, and the Washington International. Of her brilliant foals, Relko is the most successful. He won the English Derby in 1963, ridden by the French jockey Yves St Martin, the Coronation Cup at Epsom in 1964, and his French victories include the Two Thousand Guineas, the Prix Ganay, the Prix Royal Oak, and the Grand Prix de St Cloud.

A shadow fell over Relko's Derby victory when a routine test revealed the presence of 'a substance other than a normal nutrient' in his blood. An announcement three months after the race in the *Racing Calendar*, the official publication of the Jockey Club, said that the Stewards of the Jockey Club 'were not sure satisfied [*sic*] that the substance was administered with the intention of increasing Relko's speed or improving its stamina, courage, or conduct in the race'. A further inquiry, into which the police were brought, resulted in this later report in the *Calendar*: 'The Stewards of the Jockey Club, having considered the report on their further inquiries, are satisfied that the trainer and his employees have no case

to answer under Rule 102(11). They found no evidence which
would justify a disqualification of Relko under Rule 66(c).'
Thus the name of Bikini's nephew was cleared. Had the
Derby hearing gone against him, he would not have been
standing at Lavington at £3,000 a mare.

For February, March, and April life at Lavington for
Sunsuit and Bikini was a daily routine of paddock exercise
with the other mares and foals, with nights spent indoors
together and plenty of good food. There were slight variations: Sunsuit was after all at Lavington to be covered by
Relko. A week after giving birth to Bikini she came in season
and would, in the normal way, have been taken to the stallion
then, but because of the earliness in the year the mating was
put off.

The Rules of Racing dictate that thoroughbred horses shall
have an official birthday on January 1st, so that any born on
December 31st become technically one year old on the following day and are handicapped for many years by having to
race on equal terms with horses nearly a year older than
themselves. The gestation period for a mare is about eleven
months; but since it is not uncommon for foals to be born
two weeks before they are due, the thoroughbred mating
season does not begin in England until February 15th. Sunsuit
was not mated with Relko until her second heat after foaling,
which happened at the beginning of March. She was covered
on March 6th, and again on the 8th, in the exercise school
that also serves as the covering yard at Lavington for Relko
and the other resident stallion, Sing Sing. Then, having been
tested and found to be in foal, she was left to bring up Bikini
until she was big enough to travel back to Woodlands Stud,
Newmarket, which belongs to Lord Derby.

III

At Newmarket, a hundred and twenty miles north of Lavington, March came in with some of the worst weather of the winter. On the first there was a sharp frost, and racing at Doncaster and Warwick was cancelled because of snow; on the second several more inches fell, and many parts of the country had the coldest March night of the century. At Newmarket the temperature dropped to 21 degrees below freezing. Conditions were too bad for the mares to go out during the day, so Mick Ryan, the stud groom at Woodlands, spent his day supervising the clearing of the stable yard and the care of the mares. Each had to have a clean, thick wheat-straw bed, fresh water, and a pile of top-quality hay (clover and Bennett's grass mixed) as well as her regular feeds. The men worked with frozen fingers and faces reddened with the cold as Ryan made his rounds, checking and helping out.

The square stable yard at Woodlands has looseboxes on the west side for pregnant mares and mares visiting to be served by Newmarket stallions. On the north and east are slightly bigger nursery quarters for mares with foals, and also the barns for storing straw and fodder; on the south side there are two big foaling boxes with a sitting-up room in between. Ryan thought he might need one of the foaling boxes that night as Sundry, a fourteen-year-old bay mare belonging to Lord Derby, had bagged up and waxed, and had begun to run a little milk into her bed. Sundry was one of Ryan's favourite mares. He had delivered her himself, fifteen years before, and had attended her foalings ever since. Although highly strung, she was not normally nervous about foaling and had never given any trouble except in 1961, when she had slipped a foal prematurely. She was, Ryan said, 'a mare you couldn't help but like'.

By late afternoon it had begun to snow again heavily. At five o'clock the men went off for tea and the stable yard was quiet but for the rising wind and the snow whispering against the stable walls as the dark came early. At five thirty the muscles above Sundry's tail slackened. Ryan, making his rounds, noticed it and moved her into a big, warm foaling box, thermostatically controlled at 60 degrees. There was already a mare in the other foaling box, and the nightman kept watch over both, drying out his wet feet before the sitting-up room fire. The time passed uneventfully: Sundry, big-bellied and placid, made an occasional round of her box; as she moved, drops of milk fell from her teats into the clean straw. Outside it had stopped snowing. At eight o'clock Mick Ryan, in a rush of freezing air, looked in to see how she was doing. Much later the mare began to paw up her bed restlessly, and a light sweat broke out on her. The groom went to fetch Ryan and the two men settled down to wait for Sundry's labour to begin.

Shortly after midnight Sundry got down in her straw, rolled over on her side and groaned. Then she got up again, sweating heavily as her water bag slipped out and hung. Down she went again, groaning and labouring, straining hard at the unborn foal without success. Ryan, seeing that she was having difficulty, rolled up his sleeves to the elbows, washed his hands and arms in the sitting-up room sink and went quietly into the box to help her; but at his approach Sundry shot to her feet, eyes wide and unfocused in panic. The head and the forelegs of the foal, encased in thick white membrane, now stuck out of her vagina. For the first time in her foaling history, Sundry did not seem to know what was going on. Ryan's quiet, familiar voice made no impression on her, and she would not let him near her to help. Seeing that the mare was panicking, the man backed off to give her time to come to herself. As soon as he was out of range, Sundry threw herself sideways into the straw and the desperate labour began again.

Knowing that he could help, that he could, with the groom's help, pull on the foal's emerging forelegs as Sundry heaved to push it out, Ryan approached again. Immediately the mare shot up again, then almost instantly flung herself down. With the head and forelegs of the foal sticking out, Ryan knew that she could do herself or the foal much damage if she continued to abuse herself in this way. If she would not let herself be helped, then he must leave the panicked mare to evict the foal as best she could.

Sundry groaned and strained. She rolled almost on her back and strained again, eyes dilated with terror. Then she scrambled up and immediately threw herself down hard. More strains and groans; then, after forty-five minutes of hard labour, the foal slipped out. The two men waited until the blood had stopped pulsing through the umbilical cord before moving quickly and quietly in to strip off the thick, white amniotic sac; to cut the umbilical cord, which they sterilized with antiseptic navel powder. They lifted the foal to a corner of the box and began to dry it off with towels. Normally it would have been settled in the straw by its mother's head so that she could see it and help to lick it dry, but Sundry, exhausted and still panicky, was safer left to herself. Ryan called Colonel Adrian Scrope, the stud manager, telling him that the mare looked bad and a decision might have to be made to put her down.

It was a big foal—a colt, bay with four white stockings and a white blaze. It had, oddly, one brown eye and one—the right one—light blue, giving it a glassy, not-quite-looking-at-you expression. It was soaking wet, which made its coat look darker than it was, and its ears lay flat back on its neck in their prenatal position. It shivered all over with nerves.

Ten minutes after foaling, while her colt foal was still being dried off, Sundry heaved to her feet and broke out in a heavy sweat. As if someone had thrown a bucket of water over her, Ryan thought. She looked around once in a dazed way, then threw herself down into the straw. When the vet and the stud manager arrived a few minutes later, it took only a quick look at the exhausted old mare to see that she would shortly be dead. She sweated and groaned on the floor. Her eyes looked glassy. As she could not live and was obviously in great pain, Colonel Scrope and the vet decided together that it would be kinder to kill her instantly.

Sundry was destroyed on the spot with a humane killer. A post-mortem later showed that she had haemorrhaged internally from a burst bowel, probably caused by throwing herself to the ground when the foal was already halfway born.

When his dam's immediate death was decided, the foal was quickly carried from the box and put in the sitting-up room in the nightman's charge. His coat, after more towelling, dried out rapidly to a rather washy bay. He was to be named Laureate. His curious blue eye, called a 'wall' eye, was inherited neither from Sundry nor from his sire, Aureole. It could have been a throwback to his paternal grandsire,

Hyperion, who had chestnut eyes. At any rate, there were no wall eyes in his illustrious family tree.

The occupant of the other foaling box, who showed no immediate sign of giving birth, was moved out, and Laureate was installed as soon as the room had regained its sixty-degree temperature. Fifteen minutes old, Laureate stuck his grasshopper legs out into the straw in front of him and tried to get up. No success. He lay flat on his side for a few minutes gaining strength for a renewed effort, and then he began again, trying to get his hind legs under him to push. Thirty minutes from birth, being a strong foal, he scrambled to his feet — and pitched straight over into the straw. Undaunted, he began all over and was soon up, pitching precariously as he tried to keep his wobbly legs in balance. This he managed for a while, but then he got his hind legs too far under him and fell suddenly backwards into his bed. After a short rest he got up again. When Ryan came into the new box, grieving over the dead Sundry, he saw her son already up and swaying. He reached out and took hold of the colt's tail to steady him. Supporting Laureate's tremulous 98 pounds with his right hand, he forced his thoughts from the loss of the mare to the urgent problem of the orphan.

First, the foal had to be fed. The first milk of the mare, a honey-thick mixture called colostrum, is the most important milk for a new-born foal as it contains all of the dam's antibodies, which will immunize him against most diseases. Since some mares run milk for a week before giving birth and thus lose all their colostrum, Ryan kept a store of it, milked off mares between birth and first sucking, in the deep freeze at Woodlands to feed to new-born foals whose mothers had lost theirs. But in the present emergency there was fresh colostrum

on hand. Ryan had milked two eight-ounce bottles of it off
Sundry, some just before and some just after her death. Half
a pint of it was heated on the sitting-up room stove, given the
elbow test for blood heat, and put into a baby's bottle. Then
Ryan got Laureate into a corner to prevent him from backing
away, put an arm round the colt's neck to keep him still, and
held the teat to his lips. Talking gently to the foal, he got the
teat into his mouth and drew the bottle away from Laureate
so that he must suck to hold the teat in. With the bottle held
above his head at the height and angle of his mother's udder,
Laureate began his first meal.

IV

Though Laureate was not old enough to know he had no
mother, he needed one. Whenever possible, a thoroughbred
fostermother is found for a thoroughbred foal, as a foal will
imitate its mother's ways. If fostered by a carthorse, for
example, it may develop a carthorse action unsuitable for a
galloping racehorse. Leaving the groom to attend to the colt,
Mick Ryan returned to his house, not to sleep (though it was
after three in the morning and he had a heavy day ahead),
but to draft an advertisement for a fostermother in the
Sporting Life, the daily racing newspaper.

Laureate was fed every hour through the night and the
following day. When he had drunk all of Sundry's colostrum,
which went down in the first two feeds, he was fed eight
ounces of Ostermilk each time, mixed with glucose and lime
water. A young foal learns quickly. After the first hour
Laureate would come to the door of the box and wait to be
fed, tapping impatiently with his foot when he heard someone

approaching. To avoid any risk of his catching cold he was kept in the heated foaling box until a solution could be found to the problem of a fostermother. On the second morning after his birth he was taught to wear a lightweight head-collar, which was left on him indefinitely for ease of handling.

On March 4th, the *Sporting Life* carried an announcement that a fostermother was wanted by the Woodlands Stud at Newmarket. Gordon Powell of Lichfield saw it when he came in for lunch after a morning's work on his stud farm. Powell had a quiet, good-tempered thoroughbred mare called Jackie's Star, whose foal had just died. He got on the phone right away to Mick Ryan, who offered a service by the New-market stallion Henry VII in return for the loan of the mare.

A horsebox was sent out from Woodlands immediately, swinging west through Cambridge up the A45. It was an awful day. Icy roads made driving difficult during the four-hour journey, and heavy snow brought an early dark to the Staffordshire countryside. While the empty horsebox travelled slowly north, Jackie's Star's dead foal was carefully skinned and the complete skin, tail included, packed up in readiness for the return journey.

Jackie's Star, a heavily-built chestnut mare with a white star on her forehead, arrived at Woodlands before midnight. The skin of her dead foal was carried in the driver's cab so that she could not smell it. She had accepted the death of the foal, born prematurely, after standing over the body for three hours. The veterinary surgeon had given her a drench to get rid of the milk it had been thought she would not need. Now it was hoped that her milk supply would revive if she adopted Laureate.

Though the sound of the motor was muffled by the snow

which whispered against the window, Ryan saw the lights of the returning horsebox cut across the stable yard as it turned in at the gate. He put on an oilskin and went out to it through the rough night. The side of the horsebox was let down and Jackie's Star came docilely down the ramp into the storm and was led quickly to a clean loosebox, where she had a feed and an hour's rest in the sheltered dark before her introduction to the foal.

Meanwhile Laureate, still in the warm foaling box, was fed again from his baby bottle. When he had finished, the skin of Jackie's Star's dead foal was tied carefully over his body until he was completely covered except for his head, which was left bare. Even the dead foal's tail was tied over Laureate's, in order to get all of him as near to the smell of Jackie's Star's foal as possible. Laureate was not bothered by all this. He picked a bit of hay from a pile in the corner and chewed curiously on it with his milk teeth.

When all was ready, a little milk was obtained from Jackie's Star and rubbed onto Laureate's head as a final means of making his smell familiar to her. Jackie's Star, with a rein attached to her headcollar, was led into the foaling box. Settled down by the feed and the short rest, she took in her comfortable surroundings. Then, tightly reined in case she rejected him, the oddly garbed Laureate was brought to her to smell. This was a crucial moment. The men knew that a mare can easily turn on a strange foal and kill it, biting and kicking it or grabbing it by the neck and throwing it to the ground, then trampling on it; sometimes a mare will get an orphan foal in the corner and slam it with her hooves. But Jackie's Star didn't. She smelled Laureate long and carefully, and must have found the smell agreeable because soon she knuckered softly to him and encouraged him to poke along her side for milk. Within twenty minutes of their first meeting, she had helped the foal with pushes from her muzzle to find her udder and to take his first drink from it.

The watching men relaxed. Ryan felt reassured enough to go to bed, leaving the groom to remove the skin from Laureate two hours later and to stay up all night with a rein on the mare in case Jackie's Star should change her mind about the adoption, which she didn't. In the morning Jackie's Star and Laureate were loosed together in the foaling box as mother and child, or near enough.

V

Woodlands Stud, Newmarket, is part of the Stanley House estate, which belongs to the Earl of Derby. It is about ninety miles north of London, on the chalk ridge on the Suffolk-Cambridgeshire border, which is famous country for the breeding and training of racehorses. The Stanley estate covers about three hundred acres, including a large training establishment run by the trainer Bernard van Cutsem. It has Lord Derby's private gallops, quarters for a hundred and forty mares and foals, a stallion yard with facilities for three stallions, and a home farm. Lord Derby also has nursery quarters for mares and youngsters at Knowsley Park, his home near Liverpool.

At Woodlands, the looseboxes for mares and foals are spread out over several stable yards with an average of twenty boxes in each yard. The multi-yard arrangement means that it is never far to walk with the mares and foals to any paddock. The three stallion boxes are equipped with covering yards where the mares are served, and there are isolation boxes to quarantine horses that come down with contagious diseases. The home farm stocks seventy cows, Hereford-Aberdeen Angus cross, and three bulls; these are pastured in rotation with the horses to keep the grass sweet and evenly grazed, and also to help the ever-present problem of redworm by eating the larvae (which do not live in cattle) before they have a chance to be swallowed up by the horses, to whom they could cause very serious damage.

In 1965 the Stanley House estate was managed by Colonel Adrian Scrope, who booked the nominations for the horses, ran the farm, and had the ultimate responsibility for the welfare of every animal on the place. During the breeding season Colonel Scrope saw every mare on the stud every day, arriving at Woodlands at eight thirty in the morning for Mick Ryan's report and then starting his routine inspection. He was a first-class manager with very high standards, who would admit no excuse if anything was wrong. He demanded, and got, his own way, and could be relied upon to give a straightforward answer when called upon to make a decision. There was, as Ryan said, no messing about.

The two of them, Scrope and Ryan, had a mutual respect and trust for each other, born of thirty years of working together. Each knew just where his responsibilities began and ended, and that he could call upon the other at any time during the night or day. While the stud season lasted, Ryan always knew where Scrope could be reached if an emergency arose and that the manager would be at Woodlands within five minutes of getting a telephone call. Though Scrope was punctilious during the season, he never interfered during the July–December period when the mares and foals were not at

Woodlands; indeed, he was usually away shooting for much of this time. In this off-season period the ten permanent employees worked on the paddocks, clipped nine miles of hedges, and whitewashed and tarred the stables for the new foaling season.

Every stud groom has his own ideas about the best way of handling a mare and foal. At Woodlands, if the weather is warm and fine, a mare and foal go out together to the paddocks the day after the foal is born. But bad weather kept Jackie's Star and Laureate in the warm foaling box for several days after the adoption. 'You can't afford to take risks with a young foal,' Mick Ryan said. 'You must be *sure* it's warm.'

On Sunday, March 7th, when he was four days old, Laureate was given a routine anti-tetanus injection and was thereafter loosed in the paddocks with his fostermother and the other mares and foals whenever the weather was good enough, learning to use his legs at a trot and a canter and soon playing about with the other foals. Despite his washy colour, he was a handsome colt, big with plenty of bone. He had an independent character, being far less inclined to stick close to his dam than the other foals, and given to wandering off by himself. The weather had turned warmer; there were patches of fog in the early mornings, but by midday it was usually sunny and quite hot. Laureate's bit of dried-out navel cord, which would drop off when he was six to eight weeks old, swayed about beneath him in the spring wind.*

While Laureate was still learning to use his legs, another of

* A typical small difference of opinion between stud grooms is illustrated here. Wally Claydon says, '*Never* cut an umbilical cord in case you cut off some of the "blood transfusion" from mare to foal. The cord will break naturally at its weakest point soon after the blood has stopped flowing.' Mick Ryan, on the other hand, holds the cord in his hand so that he can feel when the blood has stopped

Lord Derby's mares, Samanda, in foal to Mossborough, began to run milk. Samanda, who was a fine-looking chestnut, was blind; as a foal she had gone through a fence with her dam and crushed both optic nerves. Her eyes looked normal enough, but she carried her head tilted to one side with her ears pricked to catch every sound, and moved with her nose reaching out to smell her way. She was pastured by herself a quarter of a mile down the road from Ryan's yard in her own paddock with a loosebox opening into it, and could find her way around perfectly, walking in and out of her stable without ever hitting the doorpost on either side. She was looked after by Dick Nicholls, the man in charge of Alcide, the resident stallion, and would come to his call from wherever she was, always moving in a straight line towards the sound. When she had no foal to follow for guidance, she kept herself in condition by plunging about on the spot; but if she heard other horses or human feet passing on the road beside her paddock she fixed on the sound and walked to the fence to smell the company go by. Though a kind, gregarious mare, Samanda had to accept isolation as another burden of her sightlessness. It would have been unfair to put her in a field with other horses, who might kick or bite when she could not see to defend herself.

On March 12th Samanda foaled a chestnut colt, Rainhill. The foaling was normal, and when it was over Nicholls put a head-slip on the foal with a bell attached so that the mare could hear where her son had got to.

---

flowing, then cuts it to be sure that it is long enough to tie. This is in case it bleeds when the foal is later struggling to get up, which quite often happens. Both men, of course, sterilize the end of the cord once it has broken, and both in principle have the same objective—seeing to it that the newborn foal receives and retains the full complement of nutrients from the placenta.

Rainhill was a big, strong colt, handsome and audacious. Samanda's blind dependence on him gave him extra assurance in the early days: where Rainhill went, Samanda followed. Since the mare suffered from claustrophobia, their loosebox door was never shut. Rainhill poked his nose outside within a few hours of his birth, liked it, and headed off into the odd new world. Out in the paddock in the warm south-west wind, he wobbled along with his dam keeping close to the tinkling of his bell. On March 15th he got his anti-tetanus shot. The sharp indignity of the needle made him squeal.

Three days later he, Laureate, and the ten other foals born so far were given identification numbers to keep their owners' records straight. Along with the identification numbers came the veterinary surgeon, who examined each foal and wrote down the individual markings for the identity papers that would remain with each for the rest of his life.

Spring

SPRING brought to Newmarket horses the worst coughing epidemic in memory. It was caused by an influenza-type virus almost unknown in England, and so the horses had little natural immunity to it. Since the virus was closely related to the one that caused the big epidemic in Miami in 1963, it was named A/Equi 2/Miami 63.

Coughing is much more serious in horses than in humans. Most of the viruses causing coughing in horses belong to the influenza group, and are caught by being inhaled into the air passages, where they set up an irritation, causing the victim to cough. Once the infection is established, other bacteria can more easily gain entrance – pneumonia or bronchitis can result if great care is not taken of the animal, and often even if it is.

When a large-scale coughing epidemic occurs, all parts of the racing industry are affected. Horses in training cannot race, and, if they are coughing, cannot even work; so potential prize-money is forfeited, though training fees continue. On the racetracks, horses that have been, or are about to be, affected by the cough may not show their true form, so the punter loses. Since breeders rely on their produce to advertise their stallions and mares on the track, they too are indirectly affected. But of all parts of the industry, the stud farms are the most vulnerable to lasting harm from the cough. If stallions are affected, so that they cannot cover mares, the birth-rate

55

may be down the following year and there may be more late foals. In mares, some cough viruses cause abortion. The hardest hit are the young foals, who have the least resistance. In them, coughing leads easily to pneumonia without a secondary infection necessarily being present. The results are sometimes fatal. Fortunately, coughing epidemics on studs are rare because of their isolation.

Virus A/Equi 2/Miami 63 proved to be the exception. Despite isolation and every possible care the disease spread like wildfire, carried by the wind, by birds, people, or by anything else that moved. Many foals caught pneumonia, and the stud hands came to dread the outward signs of very rapid breathing and a jerky movement of the chest. With the stud season at its height and the men working hard on little sleep, the additional burden of sick animals was very heavy.

Woodlands was no exception. On March 25th Samanda and two other mares were put on a powder; Alcide's temperature rose with the cough to 102 degrees, a degree above normal, and two mares missed being covered by him that day. The same evening Laureate, normally lively, became listless and stood with his head hanging down between his knees. For the first time, he didn't bother to finish all Jackie's Star's milk. By the morning he had a temperature of 104 degrees and needed an injection of antibiotics. Two other foals had temperatures. Rainhill came down with an infected navel and had to be injected along with the rest. By then all the mares were coughing, and the studmen sweated to bring the cough under control in a freak heatwave that lasted through the first week of April. By March 29th Laureate was better, and by the 31st Rainhill's cough cleared up. But there was little chance for the very young: a bay filly foaled on March

27th lasted on injections until April 6th and died despite it all.

Although Lavington, in Sussex, is more isolated, the cough was a problem there, too. It had been brought to the stud in mid-March by five French mares and had spread rapidly, as it had at every other stud in the country. Bikini, now seven weeks old, was never in danger from it, but there were worries about the younger foals and the foals who were yet to be born. Cloudy Walk, a small bay mare belonging to Dr John Burkhardt, Relko's manager, was due to drop a foal by Whistler on March 26th. When the day came and passed without her giving birth there was at first a general feeling of relief.

April came in hot and dry, but cooled during the second week to normal temperatures and showers. Cloud shadows chased each other across the brightening Lavington grass, and Cloudy Walk stayed on out in the paddocks, small and fat with pregnancy. The third week came, strong winds and snow squalls and a touch of blackthorn showing white in the hedges, and still she did not foal. Kennedy and Claydon began to worry, but the mare seemed healthy and unconcerned. Then on April 23rd, exactly four weeks from the day she should have foaled, Cloudy Walk gave birth quite easily. The offspring was a bright chestnut colt, compactly built and exceptionally nice-looking. Mountain Call, as he was named, stood out among the other foals of his age. Perhaps his extra month in the uterus had given him an advantage, but it was one that he was not to lose. Until the day when he left Lavington, two and a half months after his nursery companion, Bikini, he remained an eye-catching foal, strong and calm and with a fine gloss always on his copper coat.

II

From January to May, Mick Ryan, like all stud grooms, had his sleep interrupted by work nearly every night. Though he got very tired, he had the ability to go to sleep instantly anywhere at any time if he had a few minutes to spare, and thus he managed to keep awake during the long days of the stud season. Before breakfast each day he checked over every animal on the stud, having a look at the udder of each mare to see that her foal had sucked during the night. Mares that might be in season, depending upon the date of their last period of oestrus, were led from their looseboxes to a padded trying board where they were teased by a stallion kept especially for this purpose. The teaser was held on the other side of the board and allowed to lean over and sniff and nibble at the mare. If she reacted favourably, Ryan made a note to ask the vet to examine the state of her ovaries later in the morning. The Woodlands teaser, a magnificent, but sterile, bay Arab stallion, was ridden from yard to yard each morning by Ryan to see that all the likely mares were teased.

By eight thirty, when Colonel Scrope arrived to check the animals, a list had been drawn up of mares who needed testing for ovulation and of any sick animals or foals who needed injections. Word was passed on to the vet, who arrived daily at half past nine.

While the mares were being teased, the foals were left behind, out of sight and earshot of their dams, as Laureate found when his fostermother was led out one morning and the stable door was shut in his face. He screamed and fussed about

in his box until Jackie's Star came back, then quickly forgot
about it and settled down. Later, when she was taken off to
be served, he screamed rather longer; but since in the end
she came back he was able to forget again.

Although in the past there had been as many as four
stallions standing at Woodlands, in 1965 there was only one:
Alcide. In his younger days, Alcide had been outstanding,
although his racing career had been peculiar; often brilliant,
he had sometimes been unlucky or had simply not tried, and
was twice nobbled for the Derby (the second time by mistake).
At the beginning of his three-year-old season (1958) he
showed exceptional promise by winning the Lingfield Derby
Trial by a devastating twelve lengths. He was made a hot
favourite for the Derby, but a week before the race was found
in his stable in obvious pain. It is thought that he had been
dealt a blow which had broken a rib, but nothing was ever
proved against anyone. (At the risk of being unfair, it was the
bookmakers who gained most if Alcide was kept out of the
Derby, since a great deal of money had been staked on him.
His owner, Sir Humphrey de Trafford, had most to lose:
winning the Derby would have abundantly increased Alcide's
value at stud.)

Alcide had fully recovered by August of 1958. He won the
Great Voltigeur Stakes at York by a dozen lengths, and
followed it up with a storming eight-length win in the St
Leger. He stayed in training as a four-year-old. Security
precautions in the late 1950s were not nearly as tight as they
are today, and three days before the 1959 Derby Alcide was
found wandering loose by the paddocks near his stable yard,
with nothing to prevent him from getting onto a busy main
road and possible destruction. He had been 'got at' again:

someone had opened his stable door, probably mistaking him
for that year's Derby favourite, Parthia, who was stabled
three doors down. Alcide's racing career finished in a blaze
of glory. He won the King George VI and Queen Elizabeth
Stakes at Ascot and retired, having won more than £56,000
in prize money.

Upon his retirement from racing, Alcide was syndicated as
a stallion into forty shares at £8,000 each. This meant that
the forty shareholders had the right to send one mare each to
Alcide every year, or alternatively to sell the nomination for
that year for the going price of £2,500, which did not guaran-
tee that the visiting mare would be got in foal. The cost of
keeping the stallion – his feed, stud maintenance, the stallion
man's salary, a secretary's salary, advertising and veterinary
bills – was £3,000 to £4,000 a year.

Alcide had his own quarters – a loosebox, a covering yard
and paddocks – away from the mares on the home farm at
Woodlands. He was turned out for exercise in all weathers
except when he was in for covering. A stallion must be fit and
hard and healthy, and Alcide preferred his freedom to being
exercised on the roads or on the lunge-rein, a long lead at the
end of which the horse runs in a circle. If led out for exercise
he reared up and fought, but loosed in his paddock he kept
himself fit with a circus-horse display of galloping and rearing.
Like many stallions, he was dangerous when loose. He had a
strong sense of territory, and gave every sign of a readiness to
defend the area he thought of as his own. Dick Nicholls
would approach him in the paddock, warily, but visitors were
warned to stay behind the gate for their own safety. Yet
Alcide was beautifully behaved in his loosebox, provided that
he was treated with respect.

Alcide was usually brought in for mating at 10 a.m. and 3 p.m., but if he had three mares to cover — which depended upon who happened to be in season — his work would be at 7 a.m., midday, and 6 p.m. Mares, their tails bandaged and their backsides sponged down, were led down the road to his covering yard, usually whinnying for the foals they had left behind and not aware of where they were being taken. Introduced to Alcide across the trying board in the peat-floored covering school, they would get the idea and mostly settle down. Really difficult mares, frightened maidens for instance, needed working over by the teaser to warm them up, since Alcide would not bother with mares who were not willing. Whether difficult or not, all mares were fitted with double-soled felt boots on the hind feet in case they should lash out at the valuable stallion.

Alcide was an irregular mater — sometimes the whole thing was over in ten minutes, but at other times it took an hour or more if he was not much interested. Then he would hang around looking bored and resting one foot, wasting everybody's time. Four men would be present: Mick Ryan, who was there to see that all went smoothly and that ejaculation occurred; Nicholls, the stallion man, controlling Alcide; another man to hold the mare, and a spare man in case of trouble. When Alcide began to show signs of action, one of the mare's forelegs would be held up to prevent her from moving away. Often a twitch — a piece of string twisted tightly around her upper lip — was put on her to distract her attention. At the last moment Ryan took hold of the mare's tail and pulled it sideways out of the way; then, as the stallion's body rose to mount her, her held-up foreleg was released to allow her to keep her balance under Alcide's added weight. Often the great penis of the stallion was guided into the mare's vagina by the groom, the horse seeming not to notice the human interference. 'Flagging' of the stallion's tail showed when ejaculation was occurring, a twitch of his tail upwards accompanying each pulsation.

When it was all over, stallion and mare would be allowed to stay in position until Alcide was ready to dismount. Then both horses were quickly turned so that they could not kick each other or any of the attendant men, and walked separately back to their quarters. This unnatural and highly controlled method of mating is typical of the breeding of thoroughbred horses. The high values of the horses involved cannot be risked to the vagaries of unattended matings, in which a stallion may damage or be damaged by a mare.

After each service, Ryan would send a service card to the owner of the mare. If the mare, kept on at Woodlands, later came into oestrus again, the operation was repeated. Since mares were not necessarily got in foal at the first mating, Alcide often had to cover the same one several times.

III

By the middle of April the coughing epidemic was only beginning to come under control at Newmarket. A chestnut colt, by Match III out of Lord Derby's mare Bluecourt, was foaled at Woodlands on April 13th and was injected against the cough the same day. Gamecourt, as he was to be named, developed no signs of the disease and by April 20th was considered safe enough to be sent with his dam to visit the Queen's stallion (and Laureate's sire), Aureole, at Sandringham. On the 23rd, the day of Mountain Call's birth, Bluecourt and Gamecourt travelled back to Woodlands after a successful mating. Mick Ryan pastured them in the big home paddock, where Gamecourt played with other foals of his age beside the statue of one of the greatest horses in British racing – his ancestor Hyperion. The life-size bronze of Lord Derby's famous stallion was sculpted by John Skeaping after measurements taken from Hyperion's body following his death at Woodlands in 1960. Hyperion had been at stud there since 1935.

Hyperion, a diminutive horse of great character, won the Derby and St Leger of 1933. He stood only 15.1 hands high (five feet one inch – not much more than a pony), and as a yearling was so small that a special manger had to be built in his stable because he could not reach to eat out of one of normal height. He grew up to be the most brilliant sire in Britain, fathering the winners of 748 races worth £557,009. He was leading stallion six times (this distinction is reckoned on the amount of money won by a horse's progeny in any one year), and was twice leading sire of brood mares.

Not only was Hyperion a success as a sire of winners, he was also a begetter of animals who were remarkable at stud. Since many of his offspring were exported, his influence abroad is colossal. In North America alone, though directly responsible for the winners of only 127 races worth $610,363 (it should be taken into account that trans-Atlantic flights were not available for brood mares during much of Hyperion's stud life), Hyperion's influence is staggering. Through his sons Alibhai, Heliopolis and Khaled he had, by 1965, figured in the ancestry of 3,254 American winners, who between them had won 5,747 races worth a total of $34,494,515. Since other sons and grandsons of Hyperion had, conservatively, fathered

the winners of a further $3,500,000, his United States total in
tail male was brought close to $40,000,000 in 1965.

Nearly all of Lord Derby's horses are in some way
descended from Hyperion. Bikini, Laureate, Gamecourt, and
Rainhill all carried his blood. So did Mountain Call, the late
foal out of Cloudy Walk at Lavington.

While Gamecourt played around beside the famous statue,
Laureate, turned out with an older group of foals, was big
enough to take time out to pursue more adult interests. His
spindly forelegs bent wide apart so that his muzzle could reach
the ground, he plucked curiously at the new spring grass. In
the loosebox at night, in imitation of Jackie's Star, he picked
bits of food from the manger and chewed on them with
pleasure. Mornings and evenings he led out to the paddocks
and back quietly, following his fostermother but obedient to
the controlling hand on his lead-rope.

Rainhill, on the other hand, was alone with the blind
Samanda. He had no foals to imitate or to set an example to.
If he did not want to be caught he would squeal out with
childish temper, and if he subsequently did not feel like being
led he would try to sit down. But along with his strong will
went kindness and intelligence. He would come to the fence
to talk to visitors, pricking his ears with friendly interest; or,
with a burst of exuberance, would show off with a flat-out
gallop round the paddock, stretching himself to the limit of
his speed. His enthusiasm for galloping impressed the men
around the stud. 'When it gets to be two years old I'll have a
bet on that,' Dick Nicholls said.

May came, beginning mild with a few thunder showers and
turning hot at the end of the second week with the thermo-
meter up near 80 degrees. With the covering season drawing

to an end and many of the foals fit to travel, there began to be a turnover in the numbers of mares and foals at Woodlands. Some of the forty-five mares and twenty-five foals who were on the stud in April left early in May for nursery studs where they would spend the summer. Others, belonging to Lord Derby, came back to Woodlands from visits to stallions in other parts of the country. On May 11th Sunsuit, tested in foal to Relko, arrived at Woodlands with Bikini (Mick Ryan thought the foal nice-looking, though not quite standard size), and on May 20th Lord Derby's mare Lazybones arrived back from Whitsbury Manor Stud with a three-month-old chestnut filly by Tyrone, called Indolent.

Routine problems — Laureate scoured for a while, Jackie's Star was slow to get in foal, Indolent had a dirty nose, Bikini needed treatment for worms — these minor difficulties kept most of Lord Derby's mares and foals at Woodlands for a few weeks longer. On May 25th Bikini was passed fit to travel, and the following day she and Sunsuit with four other mares left on the long journey to their nursery quarters at Knowsley Park in Lancashire. Rainhill and Gamecourt made the journey with their dams on June 14th, followed by Laureate and Jackie's Star three days later. Indolent and Lazybones were among the last to leave.

By the time every mare and foal, wormed, inoculated, tested in foal or otherwise as the case might be, had been passed fit to travel and had gone, the summer had already come to Woodlands.

Summer

KNOWSLEY PARK, the seat of the Earl of Derby, is a few miles east of Liverpool. The house, begun as a shooting lodge in the thirteenth century, was expanded by successive Lord Derbys into a huge, multi-period mansion. The grounds, a 2,600-acre walled park landscaped by Capability Brown in 1775, are very fine: there are mature trees, rich paddocks, avenues, a lake, and narrow, curving driveways leading to new and unexpected views of the land. Brown's bill for this pleasing work was £100, though he made a later charge of £84 for designing the kitchen garden and altering the grounds around the house.

There are paddocks in the middle of the estate round the house, but most of the stud is on the south side. The paddocks, sheltered by thick belts of trees, are fenced mainly with larch posts-and-rails; but there are also eleven walled paddocks, each an acre big, which are perfect for very young or excitable horses because the walls are too high to be seen over or to jump. Since the local water is soft, a plant has been installed that filters lime into the water troughs in the paddocks to get a balance of calcium in the horses' drinking water. Cattle graze behind the horses, and farmyard manure is spread every fourth year. Early each spring, the grass is harrowed and rolled and limed according to expert advice.

Into this well-tended nursery, in batches, came Lord Derby's mares and foals from Newmarket. Colin Dive, the

Knowsley stud groom, was glad to see them back. He knew all the mares already and was curious to see the foals they had produced. Sunsuit, the big good-looking chestnut with wide-set eyes, was the first to arrive. Her sturdy bay daughter, Bikini, seemed unbothered by the long journey and the new surroundings. A high-class first foal, Dive thought, pleased.

Next came Bluecourt and Gamecourt, Samanda and Rainhill. Bluecourt was another good mare who, Dive hoped, would produce winners. Her other foals had been the quietest he had ever handled. Although he thought Gamecourt rather a small colt with nothing inspiring about him, Dive had personal reasons for liking him: he had always thought highly of mares by Court Martial and had been fond of Equestrienne, Bluecourt's first foal; moreover, his father-in-law was stallion man to Match III, Gamecourt's sire.

Rainhill, the chestnut colt with the white hind sock, looked strong enough, Dive thought, although very upright on the fetlock joints. He had straight ankles, rather than the springy, sloping joints desirable in a racehorse; but it would not necessarily be a handicap. Rainhill had a perfect mother in Samanda, who always had plenty of milk and was extremely kind to her offspring. Dive watched in admiration as the healthy, gentle mare came confidently down the ramp from the horsebox. If anyone had doubts about the kindness of keeping a blind mare, a few days with Samanda would convince them that she led a perfectly happy and all but normal life.

Laureate and Jackie's Star arrived next. Dive thought Laureate had rather a washy colour, was a bit leggy and a little flat-sided. But he was nonetheless the stud groom's pick of the foals, mainly because of the record of his dam, Sundry, for breeding good winners. Every foal Sundry had bred had won races, and Dive thought her the best mare he had handled for Lord Derby. Her foals were always very honest, treating humans with an admirable directness and performing work required of them in a straightforward way, and Sundry herself had never been any trouble. He had been proud of her; she had always carried a wonderful coat, and he remembered how distressed he had been when a cut on the upper eyelid had slightly disfigured her. He missed Sundry, and he knew that other grooms would miss her, too.

Lastly, on July 1st, came Lazybones and Indolent. Indolent was a nice chestnut, very pleasing as a first foal. Dive hoped she would not take after Lazybones, who was inclined to be short-tempered. Preferring always to mind her own business, Lazybones was not above laying back her ears and using her teeth if interfered with. But she was a nice-looking mare from a family that produced stock with plenty of girth. Dive thought her line would one day provide a good winner. Look Sharp, Lazybones's half-brother, he remembered as very promising until troubled with his feet.

Dive's first problem with the newcomers was accommodation. For that he had planned ahead. He liked to wean foals from their dams at as near to six months old as possible, and since weaned foals would have only each other for company, his practice was to run mares with foals of similar age together so that when the foals were at first taken from their mothers they would at least be among friends. Thus the two earliest foals, Bikini and Indolent, were pastured in a different paddock from Laureate and Gamecourt. Rainhill, of course, was kept separate with Samanda.

The routine for all was the same. Except for Samanda and Rainhill, who were never shut in (Colin Dive knew about the claustrophobia), the mares and foals were brought in to the stables at night. The day began for them at seven thirty every morning with a feed of about five pounds of oats in each manger. The mares ate most of this, the foals sometimes sticking their noses into the oats alongside their mothers' heads. Gamecourt, the youngest, was not yet greatly interested in hard food. Bikini, the oldest and greediest, ate competitively and hungrily from Sunsuit's manger.

Before going out to the paddocks, usually at about eight o'clock, they were all brushed over. Healthy animals who are out at grass do not need brushing for reasons of health or hygiene; Dive's purpose was to accustom the foals to being handled. The lesson was pointless unless the foals were made to behave properly. Careless handling of the foal and the brush would have taught bad stable manners, which are worse than no stable manners at all. Dive had it organized so that there were two men to each foal — one to hold it and teach it to stand properly, and the other to brush away quietly with a soft body-brush.

The work did not take long, but the time was well spent. Bad manners in a foal are not a serious nuisance, because the animal is so small, but in a year's time the same manners would be unpleasant, if not dangerous. Dive knew that a disposition towards bad behaviour should be straightened out as early as possible. Indolent, for example, needed correction. She showed signs of a temperament very much like her dam's, laying back her baby ears if she did not feel like being groomed and quite ready to take a nip with her sharp little teeth. Bikini, impatient like Sunsuit, got cross and fidgety if held for any length of time, though she was normally very quiet in the box.

II

Sunrise came before 5 a.m., but the dew was still on the grass when the mares and foals went out each morning. In the paddocks they stood broadside on to catch the early sun, the foals' short tails flicking inadequately to keep off the flies, each head near the rump of its dam to profit from the surer switching of her tail. When the sun was high and hot they gathered in the shade under the trees, dozing with closed eyes and hanging heads. In the cooler parts of the day they grazed, the foals playing around their dams or lying flat out on their sides asleep in the grass.

At four o'clock the men came to bring them in. They were no trouble to catch. The mares, knowing why the men had come, were usually ready waiting; the foals copied their mothers. Sometimes a foal would slip behind its dam and dance away on the far side out of reach, but it soon came back to hand. Lead-ropes were clipped on, and the line of mares and foals – one man leading each animal (all part of the training) – headed towards the stables.

Evening feeds were ready for them in the looseboxes. Each manger held seven or eight pounds of oats, mixed with three pounds of damp bran. The foals muzzled into their mothers' feeds according to the appetite of each. Later, with as much good hay as they could eat, they bedded down on clean wheat-straw for the night.

Towards the end of the first week of July the weather turned colder, with heavy rain and thunder and some flooding. As the foals were all healthy, they went out each day no matter what the weather was like. Gamecourt, the smallest,

stayed fairly close to Bluecourt at pasture, but the bigger
Laureate stuck to his early habit of independence. Though he
fed at normal intervals from Jackie's Star, he spent most of
his time at grass away from her.

Rainhill and Samanda stayed close together most of the
time, although whether this was because the mare liked to be
near the sound of her son's bell or was of the colt's choosing
was uncertain. They had one of the walled paddocks to
themselves, with a large loosebox left open for them to run in
and out of as they pleased. Samanda and Rainhill chose to
spend most nights out in the grass, using the stable mainly
to get out of the midday heat and flies or as a shelter from bad
weather. Although, because of Samanda's claustrophobia, her
foals slept out from a few days old, Dive found that they
rarely suffered from any of the common foal illnesses such as
scours or running noses. He attributed this to their lack of
exposure to disease, and unfortunately this theory proved
largely true. Samanda's foals often caught these ailments soon
after weaning, when they ran with others for the first time.

At least three times a day Dive went to see Samanda. He
had to go twice anyway to feed her, but the extra visits were
made to give her a few minutes' fuss, a break in the monotony
of being on her own. He had cared for her all her life and was
much attached to her. Samanda always came to his call, ears
pricked towards the sound of his voice. Rainhill's bell tinkled
as he galloped in circles around her or ran ahead to be first to
meet the man.

III

The summer days grew shorter. One evening early in August,

when she was six months old, Bikini's life was abruptly changed. The evening began as usual. She was brought up from the paddock on her lead-rope, with Sunsuit walking close behind, and was led into their loosebox for the night. But as soon as she was in, the door was shut between her and her dam. The groom led her over to the manger, scooping up a handful of oats and offering them to her; then he took off the lead-rope, gave her a pat and left. Always a good eater, Bikini stuck her face into the feed. But tonight there was something odd – she was the only one eating. With her mouth full she turned her head to look for Sunsuit, but there was no one else in the box and both the stable doors were shut. She called out for her mother and was answered faintly by Sunsuit, who was being led away out of earshot. Bikini rushed to the door, whinnying frantically. A reply, very far away, came back once from her dam; then there were no more answers.

Bikini paced up and down the outer wall of her box, calling out urgently. In the next-door stable, Indolent was going through the same thing with much more anxiety and noise. Except for brief forgotten periods when their dams were being teased or covered, neither filly had been alone before. The un-self-confident Indolent took it badly, but Bikini's whinnies became less agitated as the evening wore on. Hunger got to her and she finished up all the food in the manger, licking the bowl clean as she always did. After a while she lay down in the straw and dozed through Indolent's continued calls, which were getting rather hoarse. In the morning the doors were opened at the usual time, the men came in with feeds, and foals were held and brushed as they had been every morning when their dams were there. Bikini had settled down extremely well, but Indolent had gashed her head on a door fitting during the night and needed attention. Though the cut was not deep enough to need stitching, she had given her head enough of a bang to leave a small, permanent bump on her forehead.

When Indolent had been patched up, the fillies were led out to pasture. Still looking for Lazybones, Indolent set off at a gallop along the paddock fence. She completed three sides of the field and came face to face with Bikini. Both foals stopped dead, then they snorted, went up on their hind legs and began to box. Indolent quickly dropped to the ground and snaked in a nip at Bikini's round belly. Leaning on the paddock gate, Dive smiled as he watched the fillies at play. They had weaned wonderfully well.

Indolent took another day to settle down completely, but was from then on a perfect animal to handle. Bikini, always independent and previously often away from her dam for better grass on the other side of the paddock, adjusted instantly to life without Sunsuit. She was, if anything, over-friendly to people, and would follow visitors to the paddock as closely as a well-trained dog. The grooms tried to discourage this habit, which could become a nuisance later on when Bikini would be expected to behave like a racehorse, not a family pet.

Apart from a kick on the near hock, which lamed her for four days at the beginning of September, Bikini was no further trouble. She was especially good about eating, never leaving a particle of food in her manger even when extras, such as worm control powders or cod-liver oil, were added to it.

The early September mornings were misty. The sun broke through at Knowsley on trees beginning to turn colour.

Later in the month, swallows started to line up on the telegraph wires for migration and the nights were full of shooting
stars. Jackie's Star had little milk, despite the addition of
milk powder to her feeds, and Dive decided that the time had
come to wean Laureate.

Rainhill, too, had to be separated from his mother. The
stud groom always weaned Samanda's foals early to give them
a chance to develop with other foals. Rainhill had dis-
advantages to overcome at weaning; he had never been shut
in at night, had never been bullied or kicked at by other foals
or mares and so had not learned the art of getting out of the
way quickly. Nor could he turn as sharply as foals that had
galloped freely in numbers. Being intelligent and sensitive,
however, he learned quickly from the self-sufficient Laureate,
and had made up his lost ground long before Gamecourt,
the youngest, joined them in the weanling paddock.

But by then other changes had occurred at Knowsley.
During the autumn most of the horses would leave the stud.
The mares went to Ireland or back to Woodlands for the
winter, or were sent late in the year to the studs where they
would be mated. Yearlings who had summered at Knowsley
were sent into training at Newmarket. Lord Derby's foals,
when fully weaned, went to Ireland to get the advantage of
sweeter grass than could be had in the industrial fallout area
around Liverpool.

Much of the grassland in Ireland has never been ploughed.
This 'old' grass is generally thought to be better because there
is a natural selection of 'weeds' in the pasture. Some of these,
such as plantain, root deep down in the soil and bring up
trace elements which provide animals with a balanced diet.
Palatability in horses is not yet understood, and grazing sown

by humans consists mainly of the richer grasses with no allowance made for a horse's frequent need for young nettles, thistles, bramble shoots, rose-hips, or many of the other unexpected plants that make up a balanced diet. Another reason why Derby's weanlings went to Ireland was to be pastured on limestone. The calcium content is believed to be good for building bone. The differences in bone growth between horses reared on limestone and those reared elsewhere are, if any, too marginal to constitute proof, though horses reared in Ireland are legendary for their growth and health. But, as Colin Dive points out, the bone of a horse reared on limestone can never be compared with its growth had it been pastured otherwise, so the limestone theory is unprovable.

On the cloudy morning of September 10th Indolent and Bikini did not go out to the paddock as usual. At ten o'clock a horsebox drove into the yard and pulled up alongside the loading ramp, a gently sloping grassy bank that sheered off vertically at the height of the box floor. The side of the box was let down flat onto the bank and covered with straw by the driver, and the interior doors of the box were opened on either side of the ramp to make a passageway by which the horses could enter. Two mares were loaded up first, then Bikini was led from her stable, across the yard, and up the loading ramp. Facing her was what looked like an unfamiliar loosebox, and just ahead was Colin Dive, leading her as casually as if they were going down to the paddock. She hesitated a moment, but one of the grooms coming up behind took her gently by the tail and pushed her into the box. Not until she was actually inside did she become really aware of the strangeness of the place, and this was mainly because of the different sound of her hooves on the box floor. Her nostrils flared, but Dive had a handful of food and a comforting pat on the neck to offer her.

Indolent, coming next, stuck her toes in when asked to go into the strange place, and kicked out when a groom took hold of her tail to push her up from behind. Dive soothed her and let her have a look at the box. Inside there was a rustle in the straw and Bikini gave a small whinny. 'Come on, old girl,' said Dive, and she followed him quietly in.

Indolent was settled into the stall with Bikini. Dive, who stood at their heads outside the stall, held both of their lead-ropes, ready to reach in the stall and pat them if they got nervous. In the front stalls, the placid bulk of the two mares loomed in the shadowy box. One of the mares was Lazybones, but the mother-child bond had broken and Indolent did not recognize her.

The journey to Speke Airport, Liverpool, was short. When the horsebox arrived the plane was already in. It had come up from Cambridge with a mare from Newmarket and two yearlings going to Ireland to be trained. Dive left his horses in his grooms' charge and went into the airport building to see to the final arrangements.

There was an hour's wait before the Knowsley animals could be loaded up. The horses already on board the plane had to be taken off, and the stalls inside the aircraft re-arranged to get the weight of the new load evenly distributed. In the horsebox, Bikini became bored and nipped at the man holding her.

When the aircraft was ready, the two yearlings were re-loaded first. They were both colts and, although only eighteen months old, were already aware of their sex and too old to be shipped behind mares. The quieter of the two went up the ramp stiff-legged and snorting, the whites of his eyes showing nervously; the second was influenced by the first and got up on his hind legs and began to fight. When two extra men joined in against him, pushing from behind on each side with arms linked around his hindquarters, he gave up and went aboard. The Newmarket mare was loaded next, and lastly the Knowsley box was brought up to the aircraft ramp and screens were set up along both sides of the way from the horsebox to the plane's entrance. Following the two mares, both of whom were used to flying, Indolent and Bikini walked down from the box and up into the aircraft without seeing where they were being taken.

The aircraft had facilities for eight stalls — four pairs down the length of the plane, with spaces in between so the grooms could stand at the horses' heads during the flight. All the stalls could be dismantled, and frequently were when the load was changed. The partition walls were bolted together and bolted into the floor, which was carpeted with coarse matting to give the horses a good grip. The sides of the stalls were padded all around, and the roof of the aircraft was also padded to protect the horses' heads if they reared up. There were a couple of side seats for the two spare men who were always carried in case a horse got out of hand. There was also a first-aid kit with horse tranquillizers and a humane killer. The killer, though hardly ever needed, had to be carried because very occasionally a horse will go berserk in mid-air. When this happens it is better to kill the animal, however valuable, than to have it kick a hole in the side of the aircraft and endanger the flight.

Bikini and Indolent were coaxed into the last stall on the

plane and bolted in next to Lazybones. When the engines
began to turn over the two colts in the front snorted and
Indolent broke into a light nervous sweat. Dive, who was
travelling with his horses on the flight, soon soothed her down.
The plane taxied gently onto the runway and took off in a
slow ascent, while the horse handlers fed hay to the horses to
keep their ears from popping.

Horses often adapt more readily to flying than to being
driven on the road because the journey is smoother. Pilots of
these aircraft take off and land more gently than the pilots of
passenger flights, and if horse flights are subject to more
last-minute changes than passenger flights it is because the
pilot has to be sure of fine weather all the way. If an aircraft
carrying humans runs into a storm a few people may be sick,
but with horses it could mean that one or two have to be
killed.

Though a flight ticket to Ireland for a horse costs more
than the same trip by boat, it can often end up by being
cheaper because a horse that is driven to Holyhead may be
held up there for several days by rough seas, in which case
temporary accommodation expenses may outweigh the
saving on the air fare. Horse air-transport companies provide
their own experienced horse handlers to travel on the flights,
though private grooms may accompany the animals if they
wish. The normal practice is to provide one handler for each
pair of stalls, with two spare men for emergencies and to
relieve the others, who stand holding the horses throughout
the flight. Mares travelling with their foals are usually the
quietest to handle, though a young mare with her first foal
may get frightened enough to forget the foal temporarily and
could trample it. Old mares with foals have also to be care-

fully watched, especially if the foal is quite old. If the mare has become irritated by the foal and does not care for it any more, it is easy for her to crush it against the side of the stall unless somebody is there to stop her.

A horse that is upset enough by flying to rear up and get its forefeet over the front partition, which is about 4 feet 3 inches high, is not a great danger because it will usually be fussing about so much that its hind feet will soon slip, leaving it almost sitting down with only its hooves sticking over the partition. Then it is easy for the handler to push its feet back into the stall. Far from exciting the other horse in its pair, a horse that is plunging about will generally cause its neighbour to go dead quiet out of fright.

But the trip for Indolent and Bikini, like most horse flights, was uneventful. In the bright sunshine above the clouds, the steady drone of the engines and the evenness of the trip settled most of the animals into a half-sleep, from which they were woken to be fed hay on the long, misty descent into Dublin. The change in the engine note when the plane touched down and taxied across the wet tarmac made the young horses stiffen and call out nervously. When the plane stopped in front of the customs sheds, Irish officials came on board for certificates to prove that the horses had not been in contact with disease, and when they were satisfied, permission was given for the cargo to be unloaded.

Outside it was raining. Horseboxes had been driven out to the plane and the Knowsley contingent, last loaded, were first off. Dive saw them settled in the horsebox, then, knowing he would see them again in the spring, he turned without sadness to the new animals he was to take back to England.

IV

The Curragh, about thirty miles south-west of Dublin, is the racing centre of Ireland, where the Irish Sweeps Derby is run and where many horses are bred and trained. It is a rolling limestone country, richly green with thickets of gorse and aspen. Through it runs the River Liffey on its roundabout course from the Wicklow Mountains to Dublin and the sea.

A mile or two south-east of the Curragh, in the centre of County Kildare, the land rises in small, steep hills sheltered with some of the finest trees in Ireland. Here, where the grazing is excellent, where shade trees are plentiful, where the undulating ground builds muscle and agility, much of the land is used for rearing thoroughbreds. And here, in the summer of 1957, Lord Derby came to look for a nursery stud for his yearlings and for the mares he would send to Ireland to be covered by Irish stallions. He found Calverstown House Stud, 216 acres of old pasture, which had just been bought by Peter McCall.

Peter McCall was brought up with thoroughbred horses. His mother, Mrs Muriel McCall, owned the well-known Tally-Ho Stud; his uncle, Captain Sir Cecil Boyd-Rochfort, was the Queen's trainer, and his brother David was the brilliant European racing manager to Charles Engelhard, the American multi-millionaire. McCall's stud-management innovations show imagination and observation, and have resulted in such famous breeding successes as Star of India, the leading two-year-old of 1955, and the stallion High Treason, both by Court Martial from McCall's mare Eastern Grandeur.

Apart from horses, McCall's great loves are birds and trees. A keen ornithologist, he can tell any bird in Ireland by its song, and has turned Calverstown into a bird sanctuary, which goes well with his love for trees. He has planted all his favourites on his property: oak, beech, copper beech, Douglas fir, spruce, Scots pine, larch, scarlet oak. The result is beautiful. It also gives good shelter for the horses.

Calverstown House and the stables are in the centre of the estate, the house on the top of a mound and the stables a hundred yards away at the bottom of it. Next to the stables are the ivy-covered ruins of a castle, thought to be one of the old forts of the Pale that were destroyed by Cromwell. In front of it, the stream has been dammed to make a small lake.

The house faces east down the driveway to the Wicklow Mountains, fifteen miles away. On September 10th, when the sky cleared briefly in the late afternoon, McCall's pretty wife Kitty was in the garden cutting dead flowers off the rose bushes in front of the house. The horsebox from Dublin turned into the drive. She ran down the gravel path to the stables, rose petals dropping round her, to tell Peter Kelly, the stud groom.

The two mares and Indolent and Bikini were unboxed and led to their new stables. Kelly was very happy with the weanlings. 'A lovely pair of fillies,' he said to Kitty. Later, when he had fed them and bedded them down for the night, he was able to add, '*And* nice to handle.'

McCall had been absent when the fillies arrived, doing some work for the stallion Ragusa, whom he managed, but he came later in the evening to see them. Going into each stable, he looked them over carefully, and came out pleased with their nice conformation and quiet good manners. Then he looked in on the two mares, Lazybones and Riviera, who were old friends. Lazybones, who had been dozing, was annoyed when he turned on the light in her box and pushed him away with her nose. Satisfied that the horses were healthy and comfortable, McCall shut up the stables and began to think about his own dinner.

Autumn

PETER KELLY, the stud groom at Calverstown House, had been brought up a farmer and had worked with farm horses until he was twenty-seven. In 1964, because of his interest in horses, he applied to Calverstown and was sent to train under Colin Dive at Knowsley for six months. After that he took a stud grooms' course at the Irish National Stud on the Curragh, and began his work at Calverstown with very good qualifications.

Though Kelly was pleased with Bikini and Indolent, he already had in his charge a filly that he liked better: She Wolf, by Hugh Lupus out of Lord Derby's good mare, Dilettante, who was a half-sister to Bikini's dam, Sunsuit. She Wolf had been foaled on April 14th at Bruree Stud, County Limerick, where Dilettante was revisiting Hugh Lupus, and had arrived at Calverstown on June 30th. She was a bay foal with a lot of quality: tall, robust, and big-boned. On September 15th Kelly had weaned her by what he called his 'silent weaning' method: 'Say you have four mares and their foals running together. You bring them all in at night as usual, and in the morning you take away two of the mares and put them in the farthest field so their foals can't hear them shouting. Then you turn out the four foals with the two mares that are left. Next day you take the last two mares away and turn out the weanlings together. By that time the first two foals will have settled down and will keep the other two quiet.'

Weaned in this way, She Wolf had made no fuss at all. Thereafter she went out with the other weanlings at eight o'clock each morning and was brought in at four for an evening feed of about seven pounds of corn, one pound of milk powder, an ounce of mineral meal, two tablespoons of sea-weed meal (which has a high iron content and is good for building bone), and a teaspoon of halibut oil, which is six times as strong as cod-liver oil. The quantity of the feed varied with the appetite of the foal — Bikini ate more than that. At night all the horses had as much first-class hay as they could eat.

Kelly was at first bothered by the lump on Bikini's near hock that was left from the kick she had had early in September. He did not think she used the leg properly; nor did he like the way she flexed it. He got the veterinary surgeon to have a look at it and was told she would grow out of it, which she did after a time. But she still had a slight lump on her hock on October 20th, when Laureate, Gamecourt and Rainhill were flown in from Knowsley.

II

Kelly was worried. He had had a telephone call from Dublin to say that the hired horsebox carrying the Knowsley consignment would be late because one of the foals had been badly knocked about on the aircraft and arrangements were being made to stitch it up before they moved it. No one from Knowsley had travelled with the foals, and the horse handlers on the plane had not told the horsebox grooms how the accident had happened. It seemed that the foal must have panicked during the flight and slipped and been trampled by the others, who had been travelling in the same stall. Kelly could not find out how bad the injury was; nor did he know which foal had been hurt.

When the side of the horsebox was let down in Calverstown yard, Gamecourt came out first. He had been frightened and his chestnut coat was stiff with dried sweat. For a moment Kelly hoped that this was the damaged foal, because the small scratches and missing pieces of skin on Gamecourt's body were not serious. But there was nothing on him that could have needed stitching. Then Laureate was led out, bay coat gleaming. He was perfectly calm and had not a mark on him. Last, very slowly, came Rainhill. Like a horse nearly beaten to death, Kelly thought in horror. The chestnut colt could barely walk. Blood from a gaping gash under his jaw had poured down his chin, down his neck and chest and forelegs. There was blood, too, where he had been skinned on other parts of his body, most of it soaked in sweat which had run down his legs and belly and was now pooled in his hair in dirty streaks of white. He stood swaying at the exit of the horsebox, the edges of the gash in his neck still gaping open. The jugular vein had been nearly severed.

At the airport, working in the horsebox because there were no other facilities, the grooms had tried to stitch up Rainhill's neck, but the colt had been so worked up that it was impossible. They had managed to get an anti-tetanus injection into him, and had driven on to Calverstown as fast as they dared to get him proper attention.

The veterinary surgeon responded fast to McCall's emergency telephone call. The men had got Rainhill into a stable when he arrived, and the vet began at once to clean up the colt's neck round the gashed jugular vein before stitching it. When this was done he cleaned the less serious wounds and dressed them with sulphanilamide powder to help them to dry out. He finished with an injection of antibiotics and left, promising to call again in the morning.

Kelly made the colt as comfortable as he could, bringing him a warm mash while a groom gently sponged the dried blood and sweat from Rainhill's body. He noticed that the colt was very backward in his coat and thought he must anyway have been the weakest of the foals. He put an infra-red light in the box to keep him warm and closed both halves of the stable door behind him when he had finished.

He went next to see Gamecourt, who had also been given an infra-red light. The scratches on the chestnut coat had been dressed by the vet and the colt had settled down quite well and was eating. 'I thought him a bit backward in his coat and light of bone,' Kelly said later. 'But he was a nice type of animal.'

He closed the top door of Gamecourt's box and opened Laureate's. Usually the top doors of the looseboxes were left open, but these weanlings would need molly-coddling because of the shock they had been through. Laureate swung his head up out of the manger and turned his queer blue eye towards his visitor. A strong, fine-looking colt, Kelly thought; a worthy son of Sundry, the mare he had thought Lord Derby's best. A son of Aureole, too, which probably meant that he was high-mettled and difficult to handle. But Laureate had not turned a hair on the aircraft, even though he had been in the stall when the accident happened. Quite probably Rainhill had slipped under his feet and Laureate had had to trample on him; certainly he had been aware of the panic, had smelled the blood and sensed the fear, had seen his companions drenched in sweat. Yet Laureate, the most spirited foal of the lot on breeding, had arrived at Calverstown without so much as a trace of dried sweat on him.

III

For a week after his accident Rainhill was not well enough to go out with the others for exercise. His cuts and bruises had stiffened up and he moved with discomfort. The veterinary surgeon came daily to clean and dress his wounds, and the infra-red light in his box was kept on. Kelly found Rainhill sweet and shy to handle. He was surprised to see that the colt was eating an exceptional amount of salt. Rainhill spent much of his time at the salt-lick and would even take bites out of it. In a week, he got through a lump of rock salt that would have lasted most horses for three months.

But Peter McCall was not surprised by the colt's high salt consumption. In a way, Rainhill reminded him of himself. McCall had had a particularly bad experience in the war when he had been caught by the Germans. He and his fellow-prisoners had at first been mad for salt and would eat it on bread whenever they could get it, but the craving for salt had disappeared when they had settled down. McCall figured that the shock of the plane accident had exhausted the salt reserves in Rainhill's body and that his whole system now craved it.

McCall also wondered whether Rainhill had himself been responsible for his accident. Knowing that blind Samanda suffered from claustrophobia, it seemed possible that her son had caught some of his dam's fear of being shut in. He had shown no sign of this at Knowsley, but had the tight packing in with others on the plane, which would have been comforting to most foals, caused Rainhill to lose his nerve and panic?

By the end of October Rainhill had recovered sufficiently to go out to the paddocks. The weanlings had been separated according to sex, and Rainhill was pastured only with Laureate and Gamecourt. He had become rather frightened now of other horses and did not join much in their games, preferring instead to seek out and eat the wild rose-hips ripening in the hedgerows. Gamecourt and Laureate would rear up at each other and box, or race around the field bucking and kicking in the autumn gales, but Rainhill kept to himself.

As the weather got colder, the foals were brought in at noon each day so as not to waste the good food put into them. It was important to keep them warm. Let out into the crisp dawn (the light comes twenty-five minutes later in Ireland than in England) they would catch the early sun, and could be relied upon to exercise themselves through the morning. In the afternoons, had they been left out, they would have tired of their play and stood shivering at the gate waiting to be brought in, burning up in waste heat the corn they had eaten for breakfast.

The fillies were fairly good about being caught, but the men soon learned that Laureate must be caught first of the colts. If another foal was caught before him he would come up and try to bite it. Since it was not always possible to catch Laureate first, especially if it was a nice day and he felt like staying out, whoever had hold of another colt had to be ready to defend it. Laureate's sense of social precedence extended only to being caught. On no other occasion did he bully his fellows in the paddock, though he was much the strongest of the bunch.

Most of the grooms at Calverstown were a little wary of him because of his breeding and his strange eye, so Peter Kelly handled him himself. He learned that Laureate responded well to firmness and fairness, but would not stand for an affront to his pride. He would never suffer himself to be slapped for misbehaving, and would hit back instantly with a forefoot when reproved in this way.

The last of the leaves fell from the Calverstown trees. After the driest October for more than a hundred and fifty years, the rains in the late year came heavier than usual. The lake in front of the ruined castle deepened and grew muddy. On wet mornings the foals were kept in their stables. Otherwise, the routine was unvaried.

The foals' coats were left rough to protect them against the weather, but twice a week their manes and tails were brushed. All of them had done well. Gamecourt had completely recovered from his minor aeroplane injuries, and had improved so much in his general physical condition that the infra-red light in his box was turned off. By Christmas even Rainhill, who was not a brave horse, had begun to show more courage. Indolent and Bikini were the best feeders; the best-mannered were Indolent, Bikini, She Wolf, Gamecourt and Rainhill, which left proud, temperamental Laureate unpleasantly distinguished.

With the arrival of the holiday season, cars were frequent on the Calverstown drive, for the McCalls were hospitable people. On Christmas Day the sky was flat and white. In a far paddock Bikini, picking bits of dead winter grass from which most of the nourishment had gone, cast a black shadow in a white pool of rainwater. When she moved, her reflection followed in the still pond, her body foreshortened by the water and her long baby legs stretched out to stilts. In a week her childhood would be dead with the year. At midnight on December 31st she, like all the other 1965 foals, would become a yearling.

1966

Winter

IN JANUARY the yearlings turned cheeky and fresh, the colts especially so. Leading out to the paddocks, Laureate saw phantoms in the dried brown bracken. Dark green blackberry leaves fluttering in the winter wind, a bird flying out of a hedgerow, a patch of snow where the day before there had been none, were all excuses for him to whip round and snap the lead-rope tight in Peter Kelly's hands. Varying with their strength, the others were all more or less difficult to control. They had put on weight and grown well, and the good food and care had put a lovely bloom on their coats. Because they were getting hard to manage in headcollars, the time had come to bit them.

One afternoon, when Gamecourt had finished his corn lunch and was dozing, the stable door opened and his groom came in. He had in his hand a bar of steel, which he showed to the sleepy colt. By squeezing Gamecourt's cheeks on either side he got the colt's mouth open and slipped in the bit, to rest on the bare gums between the front and back teeth. The metal did not feel cold because the groom had warmed it first in his hand. The bit was buckled to Gamecourt's headcollar at both ends, so that he could not slip it out of his mouth. It had 'keys,' or players, in the centre of it – pieces of smooth metal that he could jingle up and down with his tongue. Gamecourt played with this curious toy for an hour, sucking and salivating on it and feeling the hardness of the metal on his tender gums. Then the man came back and took the bit away.

For two or three days the game was repeated every afternoon. Then the bit was put in his mouth when he was led out to pasture. For the first week he was still led, as he always had been, only by a rein attached to his headcollar. Then another rein was fastened to a leather chin-strap joining both rings of the bit and the colt was led out on two reins, though the headcollar rein was still the one most used. Gentleness on the bit rein is essential because the mouth of a young horse is easily damaged by rough use. A racehorse with a hardened mouth is likely to be a danger because an 84-pound stable lad on its back will be unable to stop it, and may find the going erratic even on a straight gallop.

One morning the horses were brought in from the paddock earlier than usual because McCall knew that the Kildare Foxhounds were meeting locally and might cross his land. He had never been troubled by foxes, even though Kitty kept hens in the orchard without any netting to protect them, but he approved of foxhunting as the fairest means of controlling a species that causes severe loss to farmers and smallholders — the alternative controls of shooting, trapping, and poisoning too often mean a painful, lingering death — and as the only method of pest control that promotes the survival of the fittest.

He had been wise to shut up his animals. In mid-afternoon the hunted fox came bounding on to the Calverstown land and went to ground in a drain in front of the ruined castle. The McCalls and Peter Kelly came out to watch the hounds come up in a wave of black and tan and white. In the stables, the yearlings woke up and moved to the doors of their loose-boxes to listen. Muddy horsemen clattered up the drive on sweating horses, mostly too late to see the huntsman gather his hounds around him and to hear him blow the *Gone to Earth* on his horn. A Land-Rover brought up the hunt terriers, which were sent down the drain to get the quarry to leave. The fox refused to move, and the hunt was about to pack it up and leave when McCall remembered some chimney-sweeping brushes he had stored up at the house. He fetched them, and lying on his stomach on the wet ground, he poked the long brushes down the drain and induced the fox to back out on the other side.

Hounds and followers went away once more on the fresh scent for a fast roundabout hunt of twenty minutes that ended when the fox went to ground again. This time the terriers were not used to get him out. Heavy clouds had been building up from the east on a freshening wind, and the day ended in a snowstorm. Hounds and horses trotted off home in the blizzard as traces of the hunt vanished under a thin white shroud.

That night foxes visited the McCalls' orchard and took two of Kitty's hens.

II

The first months of 1966 were unusually wet. The yearlings spent many mornings in their stables, since Peter Kelly did not believe in leaving them out in the rain. They had all continued to put on weight and grow pleasingly except for Rainhill, whose progress was still too slow. Early in February Kelly began adding iron powders to his evening feed to condition his blood.

The stud season started again and McCall was often away

working as manager for the stallion Ragusa. On the neighbouring studs the first foals were being dropped, and other spring signs began to appear. Celandines bloomed in the ditches and catkins dangled from the hazelnut trees. There were lambs on the slopes of the Wicklow hills. The plumage of the wild birds became brighter and neater.

Foot care is more important in the horse than in any other domestic animal. Every day the yearlings had their feet picked up so that the soles could be scraped free of dried mud and dung with a hoofpick. Once a month a farrier came to look at their feet, rasping down the horny outer wall that had grown on each hoof, much as a human toenail will grow, and trimming rough pieces of tissue from the heel of the foot and from the spongy centre cushion that is called the 'frog'.

At the beginning of March the yearlings started to lose their winter coats. The irritation caused by the dead hairs made them roll more than usual, and they came in from the paddocks plastered with mud. The long, straight hair of the adult horse began to show in their curly foals' tails, and the last two of the six front teeth in the upper jaw came through with the change of coat. They grew in the comical fashion of young horses, shooting up tall behind, then growing to the same height in front, so that they looked sway-backed until the middle section caught up with the new height. Their legs were still disproportionately long for their bodies.

Spring

IN THE normal way, nothing very much happens to yearlings during their nursery period. It is a time of rest and growth, when as much food is packed into them as they can be made to eat, and when nothing is allowed to disturb their peace. Young racehorses start their working lives much earlier than any other kind of horse, and need a great deal of strength at a very early age. A year in a horse's life is supposed to equal four in a human's. British racehorses begin to do hard work at eighteen months old, or the human equivalent of six years. In America it is even earlier – yearlings are being ridden at fifteen months. The preceding time of pampered idleness is vital.

The warm spring days at Calverstown passed quickly and uneventfully. The yearlings' complete change of coat from winter to summer took about six weeks. Though the approach of adulthood showed in the coarser hair of their tails and manes, they still had a foal-like tendency to be lighter-coloured around the muzzle and the eyes. The summer coats of the three chestnuts were much the same colour as their winter coats, but the new coats of the bays – Laureate, She Wolf and Bikini – were noticeably lighter brown.

Lord Derby wanted the fillies back at Knowsley for the summer because he enjoyed seeing his horses around the place, and so on April 24th Bikini, Indolent, and She Wolf were boxed up and driven to Dublin airport in Peter Kelly's charge. Because of the accident to Rainhill it had become a rule that one of Lord Derby's stud grooms would always travel with his horses when they went by air so that they could be handled by people whom they knew. Colin Dive met the fillies at Dublin and took them on to Liverpool himself.

At Calverstown it was warm enough for the colts to stay out in the paddocks all day, though they were brought in for the night at four o'clock and given their evening feeds. Rainhill was still the weakest, but was putting on bone and gaining weight fast. Laureate was so strong that when he spun round, as he frequently did when being led, he lifted Peter Kelly off his feet. His behaviour towards the other two in the paddock was as good as always, except that he still would not allow another colt to be caught before him.

In May, if the weather was warm and dry enough, the colts were left out all night and fed in the field. More often they were brought in to the stables. On one such evening, when the rain wind started to blow and clouds to bank up from the south-west, Kelly and his men went down to the paddock with lead-ropes to catch the colts. Laureate had other ideas and went skittering away in the lush new grass – annoying, because everyone knew it was wiser to catch Laureate first.

Gamecourt's groom, Patsy, got hold of his more docile colt fairly easily. Laureate stopped a short distance away and turned to watch; Patsy was about to attach the lead-rope to Gamecourt's headcollar. Infuriated, Laureate came rushing up on the far side and tried to bite Gamecourt. Patsy swung the lead-rope at him to push him off and caught him a blow on the side of the neck. Laureate retaliated immediately. He came round behind Gamecourt and hit Patsy back, striking him on the right shoulder with his forefoot and bruising him all the way down the arm. Kelly grabbed hold of Laureate's headcollar and got him under control before he could do further damage, but the incident reinforced the grooms' respect for Laureate, and any hopes Kelly may have had of getting another man to handle the colt disappeared completely.

Summer

THERE are a great many flies in Ireland. In the hot weather of June and July they were sometimes so bad at Calverstown that the colts were stabled during the day to keep them out of the way of the flies, and were led out to pasture at night. Since the grass and weeds were now well up, it was no longer necessary to include minerals in the feeds that were carried down to the paddocks at the end of each warm, dry day.

In the early evenings, after the sun had set and the heat had gone off the land, the horses cropped the dew-wet grass. Thrushes sang in the hawthorn thickets on the banks of the stream. When it got quite dark the colts would usually lie down and sleep. Most mornings the men would find them standing broadside on to the early sun, their healthy coats gleaming in the light.

Rainhill had never been completely fit since his accident the year before. He had grown into a very big colt, having developed too much bone, and had a heavy frame with big knobbly knees. Since his general backwardness showed that he would almost certainly not be up to the classic races and therefore would have little future as a stallion, the veterinary surgeon advised that he should be gelded.

Gelding, as castration is called in the horse, is a very common operation. It is generally done for one of three reasons: because the colt's legs are not strong, in which case gelding is advisable because it prevents him developing a heavy, stallion's body; or because the colt is not sufficiently well-bred to earn much money at stud and would be more useful as a riding horse (mature stallions are usually too temperamental to make good riding horses); or because the colt's temperament is unreliable and removal of the stallion urge will make him more tractable. A colt so operated upon is thereafter known as a gelding. Rainhill's pedigree was good and his temperament gentle and charming, but his increasing weight was rapidly becoming more than his legs were likely to support.

He was gelded in mid-July, in a brief operation performed under local anaesthetic. He was given an injection of tranquillizer beforehand, and after it was over—the operation is very quick—was kept in his stable for a couple of days so that the wounds should be free from flies. The younger the horse is the more quickly he recovers from being gelded. Usually he feels only a little stiff and sore, but Rainhill was listless for six or seven days, an unusually long time for so young a horse. Then his spirits improved and he began again to show interest in his companions and in play.

Though Rainhill recovered physically from being gelded, his mental improvement was short-lived. He grew disinclined to play with Laureate and Gamecourt; then his pleasure in taking exercise of any sort waned and his appetite gradually slackened. He had intermittent bouts of colic (stomach pain). Kelly would find him in the field or stable lying down, his food untouched, occasionally looking round at his flanks as if trying to see what was causing the discomfort. Sometimes the pains would be sharp enough to make him roll in an effort to ease them, and once in a while he would break out in a light, patchy sweat. Kelly felt sorry for the sweet, shy gelding who so obviously lacked the courage to pull himself out of these

small difficulties. McCall wondered if Rainhill had lost the
will to live, and was saddened because he did not know how
to give him heart.

Rainhill's gradual loss of condition intensified and he began
to dehydrate. His body started to give up salt, which crusted
lightly on his coat in the sweat pockets between the legs and
at the point of the shoulder. Throughout August he deteriora-
ted steadily. While Gamecourt and Laureate ate and played
with relish, Rainhill stood about in the paddock with his head
hanging listlessly. His coat had lost its bloom and his eyes
their lustre.

One morning towards the end of August Kelly had difficulty getting Rainhill to his feet. He had come to take the
gelding out to the paddock after a wet night and found him
lying down in his loosebox. Rainhill did not stir when spoken
to, and only very reluctantly put out his forelegs to get up
when Kelly pulled on his headcollar. He seemed to be having
trouble with his front feet. Once up, he stood with his forelegs
stuck out in front and his hind legs bunched under him to
take most of his weight. Kelly ran a hand down the forelegs,
which were cool, and then felt the front feet. They were hot.

The colts went out alone that day and Rainhill stayed in his
stable. In mid-morning the veterinary surgeon came to
examine him. His diagnosis was laminitis in both front feet.

Laminitis is not very common in thoroughbreds. More
usually it is found in the heavier breeds and in ponies. The
main bone of a horse's foot, the coffin bone, is cushioned
against the horny wall of the hoof by a velvet-like membrane
that is heavily supplied with blood vessels. Laminitis, which
is extremely painful, is inflammation of this membrane.

The causes of laminitis are often not known, though it is

apt to follow any toxic condition or digestive upset. The veterinary surgeon thought that Rainhill's condition could possibly be due to an allergy, or that it might have been caused by his weight. Peter Kelly, on the other hand, wondered whether he could have picked up some kind of laminitis infection in his accident of the previous October.

Rainhill did not need encouragement to stay off his feet. His bedding was changed to peat moss, which is cool and soft, and in this he lay throughout his illness. He would not get up on his own initiative, and would usually refuse to do so when asked by Kelly or by the veterinary surgeon. His feet were so sore that he did not like to walk on them. When standing, he bunched his hind legs under his body so that they could take as much as possible of his weight. He would not permit either front foot to be picked up for cleaning, and Kelly had to pick them out when he was lying down.

Since laminitis indicates problems in blood circulation, the enriching protein was removed from Rainhill's diet and he ate only mashes and hay. His feet were hosed daily with cold water to draw off the heat.

After nearly a week the heat in Rainhill's feet subsided and standing became easier for him, but simultaneously he began wasting. Despite anti-histamine injections his body rapidly became almost skeletal. His neck and flanks got thin, the ribs stood out in his staring coat, and his eyes were dull and sunken. He no longer responded to Kelly's visits with a shy welcoming whinny, no longer nuzzled into the man's pocket for a bit of apple or carrot.

One morning early in September the horsebox was backed up to Rainhill's loosebox and the ramp let down to the stable door. It was a golden autumn, and swallows were already

massing for migration on the telephone lines. With encouragement and support from Kelly the gelding went weakly up the
ramp into the dark. Rainhill was driven to the kennels of the
Kildare Foxhounds and was there humanely destroyed. A
post-mortem revealed an aneurism — the dilation of one of the
big blood vessels of the abdominal cavity — which had been
the cause of his shocking loss of weight. When the post-
mortem had been completed, what was left of Rainhill was
boiled and fed to the hounds.

Rainhill had been put down on the advice of the veterinary
surgeon, who had wanted to cure him and could not, and with
the consent of Lord Derby, who could not bear animals to be
in pain.

II

At Knowsley the fillies had passed an idle summer. They had
been left out day and night in the walled paddocks, to take
shelter as they chose in the loosebox provided in each paddock.
They were fed in the open with as much food as they would
have had had they been stabled at night: about six pounds of
oats with a pound of bran fed damp with cod-liver oil added at
night, and in the mornings two and a half pounds of oats fed
dry. Every third week they were given a change of paddock
so that their grass was always kept fresh and well grown.
Worm control powders were a monthly routine, and so were
visits from the farrier.

Had they been ordinary horses they would not have been
expected to do much work before they were four years old,
and the idleness and the good grass would have been enough
to ensure their eventual adult strength; but because they

would be required to carry a man on their backs while they were still babies, and then to take the strain of racing when they were only two or three years old, they needed constant building up.

Visitors to the paddocks were frequent. Colin Dive appeared at least twice a day to feed and inspect the fillies, and often looked in a third time when passing on his extra visits to Samanda. The blind mare, who was summering at Knowsley, had no foal to keep her company that year; she was awaiting one by Romulus early in the spring. Lord and Lady Derby came often to the paddocks to talk to their horses, sometimes bringing with them house guests or friends who had dropped in.

The eighteenth Earl of Derby is a big, kindly man with a deep love for horses. He was born in 1918, and served with distinction throughout World War II in the Grenadier Guards. His father, Lord Stanley, died in 1938, and on the death of his grandfather in 1948 he inherited the Stanley House racing stables and the famous Stanley and Woodlands studs. Knowsley Park was part of the inheritance.

The Derby family has a great racing tradition. The famous race was named for the twelfth Earl, who had an enormous influence on racing on Epsom Downs. Racing at Epsom is recorded as far back as 1648, but the great days of racing there did not begin until towards the end of the eighteenth century. The turning point is attributed to the Derby family. In 1773 the twelfth Earl, who was only twenty-one, leased a large country house called the Oaks on the outskirts of Epsom. He was a steward for the race meetings, and he always invited a large party of friends to stay for the races. Most of the races at the time were run in heats over distances varying from two to four miles. In 1778, Lord Derby and his friends founded a mile-and-a-half race for three-year-old fillies, which they called the Oaks.

The Oaks was run for the first time in 1779. It was such a success that an additional three-year-old race, this time for colts and fillies, was planned for the following year. The two men most responsible for it were Lord Derby and Sir Charles Bunbury, the foremost racing men of their day. They tossed a coin to decide what to call the new race. Lord Derby won the toss, and the first Derby was run in 1780. Bunbury's colt, Diomed, won it. As Lord Rosebery said a century later, 'A roystering party at a country house founded two races, and named them gratefully after their host and his house, the Derby and the Oaks. Seldom has a carouse had a more permanent effect.'

The first Derby victory for the Derby family came in 1787, when the colt Sir Peter Teazle won for the twelfth Earl, who had named the horse as a compliment to his second wife. Lady Derby had made a great name for herself on the stage in the part of Lady Teazle in *The School for Scandal*.

During the nineteenth century, interest in racing varied in the Derby family. The fourteenth Earl loved the sport, but his successor was not much interested in racing or in breeding. In 1893, the sixteenth Earl, succeeding his brother, renewed the stud and racing tradition of the family. His son, the seventeenth Earl, was to become as famous in racing circles as his ancestor, the twelfth Earl.

The seventeenth Earl of Derby, born in 1865, gave much of his life to racing. Under his guidance the Stanley and Woodlands studs and stables were founded on their present lines, and under him they achieved their greatest successes. The

Derby colours – the famous black jacket, white cap – were
carried to victory (by Sansovino) in the Derby of 1924 for the
first time since 1787. The seventeenth Earl won the Derby
twice more – in 1933 with Hyperion, and in 1942 with Watling
Street. He also won the Oaks twice, the One Thousand
Guineas seven times, the Two Thousand Guineas twice, and
the St Leger six times. His most outstanding horse was of
course Hyperion, whom he bred from his great home-bred
mare, Selene. (Selene also produced for Lord Derby the
great stallions Sickle and Pharamond, who were exported to
America. Sickle's descendants include the famous sire Native
Dancer and his grandson, the brilliant Sea Bird II, easy
winner of the 1965 Derby and Prix de l'Arc de Triomphe and
arguably one of the best horses of the century.)

This great racing empire passed to the present Lord Derby
in 1948. His enthusiasm for breeding and racing is great, but
he has not yet enjoyed anything approaching the success of
his grandfather. Luck in racing is a curious thing. A trainer
who goes for months without producing a winner will
suddenly find his whole stable in form. Conversely, a top
jockey who is apparently invincible will ride fifty or a hundred
losers in succession, no matter how many trainers he rides for.
Lord Derby has bred and owned a number of good winners
but he has not so far won a classic.

He takes a great interest in his horses, and whenever possible he goes to race meetings at which he has a runner. He
visits Stanley House Stables, where his horses are trained,
about four times a year, spending several days at a time at his
house in Newmarket. He keeps brood mares and yearlings on
his Knowsley estate so that there are always horses around.
At any one time he owns twenty or more horses in training,

some fifteen to twenty brood mares with their foals, and a pro-
portionate number of yearlings, depending upon the number
foaled the year before.

Bikini, Indolent, and She Wolf were at Knowsley because
Lord Derby enjoyed having them at home. Bikini came in for a
lot of attention from visitors to the paddocks because she was
extremely fond of humans and would follow them around.
She had developed into a big, sturdy sort and was rather
bossy with the other fillies, nipping and shoving to get them
to do as she wanted. Her domineering behaviour frequently
upset She Wolf, but Indolent paid little attention to it.
Dive admired Indolent's presence of mind: he thought her
a well-behaved animal and also a well-developed one.

Towards the end of August, which had been a cool and
rainy month, the fillies began to be brought in at night. They
would soon be going into training at Newmarket, and daily
handling and grooming would make the coming change
easier for them and for the men who were to take on their
education. They were now old enough and experienced enough
to stand quietly tied up to a ring on their stable walls while
the grooms worked away on their coats and cleaned out their
feet. Dive felt that at least a month would be needed to get
them thoroughly settled into the routine of being stabled on
their own. Bikini and Indolent did not mind the nightly
separation from their companions, but She Wolf, who had
inherited a lot of nervous energy from her dam, proved quite
a problem. When first shut in she paced up and down trying
to find a way out and was upset enough to break out into a
sweat. Her uneasy behaviour continued for the first two weeks
of sleeping in, and usually went on for a couple of hours every
evening. It did not, however, affect her appetite.

Each morning the fillies were led out to the paddocks where the summer before they had been pastured with their dams. The 1966 foals of Lazybones and Sunsuit — Lazybones had produced another chestnut filly and Sunsuit another bay — had reached the weaning stage, and the small cries of their initial separation from their dams could be heard late in August. Wet weather made the swallows and house martins that had nested in the stable eaves skim down almost to the grass in pursuit of flies, but despite the rain the harvest was safely in and on clear nights distant fields glowed in orange patches as the stubble was burned off.

After a changeable start the skies of September cleared and the month was sunny and dry. Mornings were often misty, and the first leaves began to fall, but the frosts had not yet come. The horses started to lose their summer coats.

One of the last things Dive did before sending the fillies off to be trained was to take their measurements. The height of a horse is taken from the withers, the highest point of the back, just in front of the saddle, and it is reckoned in multiples of four inches, called 'hands'. At the end of her nursery period Indolent was 15.1¾ hands high, or just over 5 feet. Bikini was the shortest at 15.1, and She Wolf a rangy 15.2¾. They were all healthy and well-mannered, but they were not as impressive to look at as they would have been had they been reared with the yearling sales in mind.

III

There are two kinds of racehorse breeders: those, like Lord Derby, who breed horses to race in their own colours, and those who breed commercially in the hope of producing splendid-looking yearlings that will make a profit at the yearling sales. Yearlings who are reared to be raced by their breeders have a slight advantage over those who are bred for the sales because they do not have to be forced so early, but horses of the second category, who have had to begin their education earlier, often look more mature at the same age.

Mountain Call, the late foal by Whistler out of Cloudy Walk who was born at Lavington nearly three months after Bikini, had been bred to be sold as a yearling. He belonged to Dr John Burkhardt, one of the cleverest producers of animals for the yearling sales. In the autumn of 1966, Mountain Call looked older than any of Lord Derby's yearlings. It would be fairer to say that he looked older to the uninitiated: he had a more muscular body, carried himself better, and was less childish in his behaviour.

Much of Mountain Call's upbringing had been similar to that of Lord Derby's animals. He had stayed on at Lavington as a foal for three months until it was certain that Cloudy Walk, like Sunsuit, had been got in foal by Relko, and had then travelled with his dam to Bolton Stud, Harewood, near Leeds, for a further nursery period until he was big enough to travel to Ireland. In September 1965 Mountain Call and Cloudy Walk had been sent by horsebox to Holyhead, where they were shipped without delay to Ireland.

Dr Burkhardt's nursery quarters were at Prospect Stud, County Tipperary, which was his own property. He bought all the food himself, inspecting it personally before purchasing. Since his aim was to develop his young horses as fast as possible, corn, hay, and bran were not fed by equal weight but according to the personal preference of each animal and by the amount that it would eat. The only exception to this was that they were all fed bran, boiled oats, a little barley, and either molasses or honey. At nine or ten o'clock in the evening Dr Burkhardt's nightman went round the boxes. Any horse that had finished its feed got another bowl or more of corn to last it through the night.

Like all responsible breeders, Dr Burkhardt was very particular about his staff. He attributed the success or failure of a racehorse, unless there was something physically wrong with it, entirely to all the people who had handled it from birth. He believed that labour should be quiet, reliable, and well-trained. 'If it is,' he said, 'there should be no problems with the horses. Labour should get incentives — cash ones — for producing good animals that sell well as yearlings.'

He also had strong views about national attitudes to thoroughbred breeding. Racehorses are a valuable export commodity in many countries, and he felt that it was in a nation's interest to encourage the production of quality bloodstock. The French pay 10 per cent of a racehorse's winnings to its breeder, even though the horse might no longer be his property, and Dr Burkhardt approved of this policy. (The only condition made by the French is that the horse must be both foaled and raced in France.)

From the day of arrival at Prospect every foal had his feet picked out morning and evening to teach him manners as well as to keep him clean. Dr Burkhardt's foals were wormed for the first time at ten weeks of age through a tube up the nose into the throat. The worm powder was dissolved in water and poured into a funnel held above throat level. Worming was repeated at fourteen weeks and thereafter every two months.

Mountain Call had been an exceptional foal. He was out-standingly good-looking, and was also strong, brave, gentle and very quiet. Temperamentally he took after his dam, who was never worried by anything. He and Cloudy Walk were pastured with a mare whose colt foal, Panpiper, was also by Whistler. Panpiper was much more of a live wire than his half-brother, and when weaning time came around in October 1965 he was more deeply bothered by it.

The Prospect method of weaning was simply to move the mares a mile down the road. Mountain Call and Panpiper stayed behind in adjacent looseboxes, with a grille between them so that they could see each other. The grille was set into the wall in a corner by the mangers, so that the young horses would be encouraged to eat in competition with each other.

The colts spent over a year at Prospect. They went out to the paddocks every day, weather notwithstanding, and were brought in when they felt like it: when they had finished playing or grazing they showed it by coming to the gate or by taking shelter under the hedges. Mountain Call was a big eater, and although he enjoyed getting out to the paddocks, he was often still busy with his breakfast when his contemporaries were fretting to leave their stables.

Mountain Call and Panpiper were due to come up for auction at the Houghton Sales at Newmarket on October 15th, 1966. Preparation for the sales began at the end of August. Sales by auction are an ordeal for any horse, but they are particularly trying for a young, impatient one. During the three-day viewing period prior to the auction, the yearlings must be present for inspection by potential buyers in one of Tattersalls's well-equipped looseboxes on the auction premises. Every time a visitor shows interest, the yearling must allow his mouth to be inspected, have his feet picked out and looked at, and have his bridle put on. Next he is brought out of the box, made to stand still for inspection, and walked twenty-five yards or so while the customer faults him. All this is very boring for the horse, who will often become so sick of being led out for no apparent purpose that he will refuse to re-enter his stable.

For six weeks before the Houghton Sales, Mountain Call and Panpiper were bitted and walked into four or five strange boxes every day. Mountain Call was perfectly unperturbed by this, but Panpiper, more fretful, used to grind his teeth. They were also taught to walk out well and show themselves off, and to stand still with their weight balanced squarely on all four feet. They were lunged daily—worked in circles on a long lead to the left and to the right—which taught them to balance themselves and move well, and also filled out the muscles on their backsides so that they became plump and strong. And they were thoroughly groomed so that their coats clung shining to their skins and showed up their well-developed bodies.

On October 10th—five days before the auction—Mountain Call and Panpiper made the long journey from Ireland to Newmarket, taking the boat to Holyhead and travelling on by horsebox. The Irish Sea was kind to them, and the long journey across North Wales and diagonally south-east across England went smoothly, if slowly. By nightfall they were installed in looseboxes at Tattersalls's, too tired from travelling to worry much about the strangeness.

Tattersalls's sales facilities at Newmarket are impressive. The auction ring is housed in an octagonal building with tiers of seats going up on all sides to hold 1,500 people. Neat stable yards for the horses which are to be sold lie away to the north, west and south of the main buildings. The area to the east is used for a car park. The sales attract top-class bloodstock and buyers of all nationalities, and are often held in conjunction with one of the big Newmarket race meetings.

During the course of the three-day viewing Mountain Call was pulled out of his box by buyers more than a hundred times. His mouth was opened by many strange hands, his legs felt, and his feet picked up. Conflicting comments were passed about him. (Asked what he looked for in a young horse, one prospective buyer said, 'the head of a princess and the arse of a cook.') The weeks of training had been a good investment, however, and Mountain Call behaved equably throughout. Ironically, the man who eventually bought him did not even need to bring him out, but just looked at him in the stable. When the time came to parade before the auctioneer, Pan-piper, who was deeply fed up and showed it, just made 2,000 guineas. Mountain Call's good looks and sensible behaviour stirred up a lot of interest in the ring, and after some spirited bidding he was eventually bought by the trainer Bernard van Cutsem on behalf of Mr Isaac Kornberg for 6,200 guineas, a very good price for a yearling whose pedigree was nothing special. After the sale, he was led back to his loosebox to wait while shipment was arranged for him.

Later in the afternoon of the same day he was taken to van Cutsem's training yard—Lord Derby's Stanley House Stables at Newmarket.

Autumn

THE town of Newmarket is in a hollow. Coming in from the south on the main road from London one can see clear across the town to the chalk downs rising up on the far side. A dot like a fly on a billiard table is a racehorse at full stretch a mile away beyond the red roofs.

The inhabitants of Newmarket are mostly small, since many are employed as lightweight stable lads or have graduated, as hopes faded of ever becoming jockeys, to working on stud farms. Talk in the town pubs is incessantly of horses and of racing, past and present, and the capacity for recall of names, speeds, and dates is extraordinary. Even history exists in terms of the horse: 1939 is not the year that war broke out but the year Blue Peter won the Derby.

Newmarket is the centre of British racing, and has been so since racing became in any way organized. The beginnings of racing are so far back that they are beyond recorded history, though there are instructions for training racehorses on Hittite cuneiform tablets dated about 3,200 B.C. The first horse races on record in this country happened during the Roman occupation, and it is probable that the Romans introduced racing here. For centuries thereafter, races took place in a limited way all over the country. They were usually held on public holidays, in market places or as private matches arranged between gentlemen. It was not until the early seventeenth century, during the reign of King James I, that racing began to have any organization.

James built a palace at Newmarket, a tiny village that had caught his fancy, and visited with his Court for sporting holidays. While he preferred hunting and hawking to racing, racing was very popular in Scotland at the time and Scottish members of the Court soon established the sport at Newmarket. James recognized the military and civil importance of improving the speed and stamina of British horses, and encouraged the importation of good foreign horses to strengthen the breed.

The British thoroughbred racehorse is a very recent hybrid, having evolved with astonishing speed over two centuries, the seventeenth to the nineteenth. Its precise origins are obscure, but it is almost certainly the result of breeding the fastest native horses to imported stock. The most influential foreign breeds were the Arabians, closely followed by the Barbs (from Barbary in North Africa) and the Turks. These foundation breeds have courage, intelligence, endurance and speed, though not the exceptional turn of foot of the modern racehorse, which is taller and therefore has a longer stride.

The three most famous foundation sires of the racehorse are the Darley Arabian, who was sent to England in 1704 by Thomas Darley, the British Consul in Aleppo; the Byerley Turk, who was Colonel Byerley's battle horse; and the Godolphin Arabian, probably part of a gift of horses to the King of France from the Bey of Tunis and later acquired for Lord Godolphin's stud at Cambridge. These three great horses were all imported early in the eighteenth century.

Racing survived at Newmarket under Charles I, who was not a great racing man, and blossomed under Charles II, who

could not have been keener. Charles II founded races at
Newmarket known as Royal Plates, and liked to come and
watch the racing every summer, with Nell Gwynn kept more
or less discreetly down the road. He is the only English king
to have won a race on the flat with himself as rider. He won
the Newmarket Town Plate, a race of his own invention for the
townspeople of Newmarket. In fact, he won it twice.

With such royal patronage, the popularity of racing increased. In the mid-eighteenth century the Jockey Club,
later to become the governing body of racing, was formed.
Its most influential early member was Sir Charles Bunbury,
who, with Lord Derby, was the founder of the Derby. The
Jockey Club began as a social club for racing and horse-
breeding gentlemen, and one of its early London meeting-
places was on the premises of Mr Richard Tattersall, a
bloodstock agent, at Hyde Park Corner. Naturally, the Jockey
Club wanted a Newmarket base, and land was leased for it at
Newmarket in 1752. When Tattersalls moved to Knights-
bridge in 1865, the Jockey Club's London meetings were held
in the offices of their agents, Messrs Weatherby, in Bond
Street.

In the early days of racing the Jockey Club's power extended only to Newmarket Heath, but requests from other
racecourses to settle disputes led to the Club's agreement to
adjudicate on courses where Newmarket Rules were en-
forced. Ultimately, all races on British flat courses were
united under the sole authority of the Jockey Club, while
reciprocal agreements were made with nearly every foreign
country in which racing takes place. In 1968 the Jockey Club
and the National Hunt Committee, which controls British
steeplechasing, were amalgamated and called the Jockey Club

(incorporating the National Hunt Committee). Messrs Weatherby and Sons, agents to the Jockey Club since 1770, retained their enormous administrative job in the new organization, but the Jockey Club's personal responsibility for the administration of Newmarket passed, after more than two centuries, to the Newmarket Estates and Property Company.

Throughout this entire period, Newmarket has kept its supremacy as the headquarters of British racing. It is a town given over entirely to the breeding, training, and racing of horses.

The Newmarket racecourse lies to the south-west of the town, on a broad expanse of level ground stretching away towards Cambridge and the Fen country. It is called the Rowley Mile, in honour of Charles II, who was nicknamed 'Old Rowley' after his favourite hack. An additional course, called the July Course, has been made south of the main course and is separated from it by a 37-yard-wide earthwork called the Devil's Dyke, believed to have been built in the Iron Age. Both of these courses were laid out before racing was thought of as a spectator sport, and in longer races the first mile of the track is out of sight of the grandstands. The Sefton Course, a rough oval two miles around that finishes with the last five furlongs of the Rowley Mile and shares the same facilities for horses and racegoers, is always visible from the stands. It was opened in 1958, and is named for Lord Sefton, a former Senior Steward of the Jockey Club who did much for the modernization of Newmarket racing.

In and around the town are the racing stables, where over two thousand horses are trained each year at an annual average cost of £1,850 each to the owners. Further out, lapping round the edges of the training grounds and racecourses, are the studs.

The principal training grounds at Newmarket are on the north-east side of the town, ideal because the downs rise and fall in gradual slopes that put muscle on a horse and also because the chalk soil drains well and the ground is almost always good to gallop over. Belts of trees, mostly beeches, give some protection from the stinging winter wind, which comes unchecked by high ground straight from the Ural Mountains. More training gallops are provided on the south, or racecourse, side of the town, where practice jumps for steeplechasers have been built on the Links, so-called because the land also doubles as a golf course.

Most of the racehorse trainers do not have their own private gallops. Instead, they pay fees to use the public gallops, which are kept neatly trimmed and rolled by gallops men, who also tread back the pieces of turf that have been churned up by flying hooves. White discs mark out the path for each morning's work, and these are moved daily so that no strip of the turf becomes unduly worn. 'Ploughed' gallops – strips of deep, fine soil – run side by side with some of the major turf gallops, offering an alternative form of exercise. Steady canters on the plough, which is heavy going, give the horses a good, muscle-building workout and teach them to use their feet carefully. After each cantering session, the gallops men rake the plough back neat and smooth.

There is always perfect galloping ground at Newmarket. In high summer, when the ground has dried out and is too hard to work on without jarring the horses' legs, thousands of gallons of water are poured on to selected strips of turf to give a perfect, resilient surface. Trainers who work their horses on these watered gallops are charged £2 a day for each horse, which most consider very fair.

Stanley House Stables, the racing home of Lord Derby's horses, lies on the north side of the town, a little way up the Bury Road on the left. It is approached through a long avenue of lime trees, which screens the stable yards from the road. Stanley House itself, Lord Derby's home when he is in Newmarket, is a big, red-brick Victorian building facing north onto the stable yards. The main stable block, which stands on three sides of a gravelled yard, is built like an E with the centre bar missing and has accommodation for thirty-one horses on the north and east sides and for sixteen stable lads in a hostel on the west side. Tons of hay, corn, and straw are stored in lofts under the sloping red roof, which runs all the way round the building. Running parallel to the north side of the yard and behind it is a row of twenty more stables. There are another thirty or so looseboxes in the Sefton Yard, two or three hundred yards away at the back, but these are not used if there is any room left in the main stabling block because they are too far away for convenient supervision by the trainer and head lad. The Sefton Yard is at its most useful in September and October when the yearlings come to be broken in, because the change of environment and way of life for these young horses often brings on coughs and colds which can be kept away from horses in the main yard who are still racing.

The trainer at Stanley House is Bernard van Cutsem, one of the shrewdest and most competent men in racing.

II

Laureate and Gamecourt left Calverstown in mid-September

to go into training at Stanley House. Peter Kelly was to travel with them on the flight to Cambridge, the nearest airport to Newmarket. Gamecourt, who possibly remembered his former excruciating flight with Rainhill, snorted and sweated nervously when the aircraft engines started up at Dublin. Shortly after take-off he became over-excited and began plunging about, eventually slipping and falling down in his stall. The pilot headed back for Ireland, whereupon Gamecourt got up, not much shaken and apparently unharmed except for a small scratch. The plane turned again and flew on to Cambridge.

Mick Ryan, who had come in a horsebox to meet the flight, had no trouble recognizing Laureate, because of the odd wall eye and the flashy white legs. The air of confidence that he had remembered in him as a foal was more marked than ever. Gamecourt was a little tricky about being loaded into the horsebox and sweated slightly, from nerves, on the shoulders and around the flanks, but the twelve-mile journey to Newmarket passed smoothly enough. The colts were unloaded in the Sefton Yard, where looseboxes had been made ready for them, and were given a warm mash of bran and oats to settle them down. Ryan then went back to Woodlands, his assignment as horse escort completed. His normal job as a stud groom did not involve the training of horses.

It was by then only four o'clock in the afternoon, half an hour before the evening stable routine was due to begin, and so Stanley Warren, who was van Cutsem's head lad and the man responsible for the welfare of all the horses and for supervision of the stable hands, was free to come down and look at the new arrivals. He did this automatically, to see that they had travelled safely and had not taken any knocks on the journey. The trainer himself, who was away at a race meeting for the afternoon, would come and look them over when he got home.

Warren was delighted with Laureate at first sight. 'He's got class written all over him,' he said later to his wife, Pat – but Gamecourt did not impress him as much, being not so robust-looking. The scratch he had sustained on the plane was slight, but Warren anyway called in the vet for a precautionary anti-tetanus injection.

Since a racing stable as successful as Bernard van Cutsem's has a great number of yearlings sent to it each year to be trained, the initial breaking-in process is, where possible, done in two batches. The yearling colts, being slightly stronger than the fillies, come in first and a week or two of the most difficult elementary lessons are given to them before the fillies come to be broken in. This applies mainly to home-bred animals; yearlings who are bought at the sales or privately arrive sporadically, whenever they happen to be purchased.

The head lad's first responsibility is to the horses who are actually racing, and since the flat-racing season in England does not finish until early in November Stan Warren would have little to do with Laureate and Gamecourt and the other yearlings in their most elementary stages of instruction.

A special kind of patience and understanding is needed in a man who breaks in young horses. His quality is as valuable and permanently effective as that of a first-rate primary-school teacher. In 1966 Bob Bland was the man in charge of the yearlings at Stanley House. He was assisted by experienced men from the main yard who had shown an aptitude with yearlings and who were also light enough to ride them. These men weighed between 112 and 126 pounds.

The matter of not overloading the yearlings was most important. Permanent damage can be done to the spines of young horses who are made to carry too much weight too early. When it is too late, the inexplicable failure of apparently healthy racehorses is often discovered to have been due to fusion of vertebrae in the spine. Oddly, such handicaps do not necessarily impair the performance of the horse: the skeletons of famous racehorses in the Natural History Museum, London, show that some of the greatest races were won with damaged backs. A widespread myth that Eclipse, the outstanding, never-beaten racehorse of the last part of the eighteenth century, had a perfect spine because he was not ridden until he was four years old is quoted by a number of British trainers as a reason for not overloading yearlings. The damage to Eclipse, however, differs from the damage done to other famous horses who were broken in earlier.

Here is an extract from a letter from A. W. Gentry of the Department of Zoology at the Natural History Museum, London:

Eclipse shows fusion at the edges of the neural spines between the last two thoracic vertebrae. There is also fusion of these vertebrae over the whole area of their articulations (zygapophyses). Fusion of the zygapophyseal region and the transverse processes can also be seen on the last two or three lumbar vertebrae. The skeleton of William III [winner of the Gold Cup in 1902] is like that of Eclipse.

Four other racehorses (Persimmon, St Frusquin, St Simon, Brown Jack) show the same sort of developments, but they have extra articular surfaces developed at the top of the neural spines in the centre of the back.

The more localized and somewhat different damage to Eclipse may be because he was not raced until 1769 when he was five years old. But I don't know about William III, and other explanations are of course possible.

It is stated on the label for Eclipse, and I have seen it in a book, that his spine is undamaged, but this is not true.

Initially, Laureate and Gamecourt and the four other colts in the same stage of training had their richer foods drastically cut down. They had all been used to playing all day in the paddocks, and the change from free movement to standing quietly in the stable for 22½ hours or more a day would have made them impossibly frisky to handle had their high corn intake been maintained. Unaccustomed inactivity coupled with a high protein intake would also have caused their legs to swell up. They were fed all the hay they could eat, but the corn ration was cut to about eight pounds a day each – a bowl of corn and chaff in the morning and a relaxing corn-and-bran mash at night. Except for their second day in the Sefton Yard, grass was also excluded from their diet.

On the morning after their arrival at Newmarket the yearlings were led out to pick grass in the smaller paddocks while they got used to their new surroundings and to the unfamiliar people who were handling them. They all wore bridles because they were mostly strongheaded, and all were big enough to be difficult to manage if they felt like making trouble. The Stanley House paddocks are on flat ground, enclosed with four-rail fencing and bordered by sheltering belts of trees, which were turning colour in the late September air. Laureate felt well enough to shy and prance about when a bird rustled the newly-fallen leaves. He was marked out from the start as a potential troublemaker: many of the staff at Stanley House had known Sundry, his dam, and Alcalde, his useful half-brother by Alcide. They knew they could expect problems with Laureate. 'Sundry was a bit wayward,' Stan Warren explained. 'Her offspring were always difficult to ride. Alcalde was tricky, and his rider always had to sit tight. In addition, Laureate was by Aureole, which made the lads a bit tense with him. So we thought we'd better pay extra attention to breaking him in.'

Despite the forebodings, Laureate took to his lessons easily and with interest. It was Gamecourt who was nervous about his new duties. Bob Bland tacked him up with a bridle and a headcollar over it and led him out to a small paddock to teach him to lunge. He fastened a rein to the headcollar on the right side of the noseband, passing it round Gamecourt's nose and through rings on the left side and back of the headcollar so that, while apparently the colt was being led from the back of his head, the controlling pressure was on his nose. Another rein, buckled to a coupling joining the two bit rings behind Gamecourt's chin, was purely a safety device in case he got out of hand. With the help of a groom to lead the colt by the head, Bland stood at a distance of about five yards holding the lunge reins and giving out commands such as 'Walk on', 'Trot', 'Canter', and 'Stand', while Gamecourt and the man controlling him moved anti-clockwise in a circle. The actions were followed up by a long whip held in Bland's right hand, not intended for punishment but as an extra indication of the direction in which Gamecourt was supposed to move. Once or twice when he baulked the whip was flicked sharply across his hind legs. Racehorses are intelligent and Gamecourt, although unsure of himself, soon learned what was required of him. After about half an hour, when he had begun to go steadily and comfortably, the lesson was stopped so that he did not get bored.

The following morning the lesson was repeated. Laureate had by then advanced to learning to lunge to the right hand, but Gamecourt needed the extra day of work to the left before he became sufficiently settled to start the second stage. When both colts would lunge easily to either hand without the help of a man to lead them, the first stages of learning to wear a saddle were begun.

The new piece of equipment they had to get used to was called a roller. It was a strap round the middle, running behind the front legs and over the back where the saddle would later be put. The roller was held from slipping back by a breast girth, which was a loose strap round the front of the shoulders, and a crupper ran backwards and under the top of the tail. Since it was the first time that anything had been tied round his body, Gamecourt's head was held by two men while a third very quietly fitted the roller over his back and clipped the breast girth in place. Then he girthed the roller just tight enough to hold.

All of the men stood clear. Bland, who had hold of the lunge rein, gave the command: 'Walk on.' Gamecourt began to move and became for the first time aware of the light constriction of the roller, so slight that he had not noticed it when standing still. He was appalled: all his instincts told him that the only thing he would ever find on his back would be an enemy. He let out a loud, deep-throated honking noise and leaped stiff-legged into the air. Then he began to buck and plunge like a bronco. He could not get rid of the roller. Suddenly he shot forward in a wild gallop, running crazily on the end of the lunge rein. Bland leaned hard against him, both feet dug into the turf to hold him to a circle. After a time he tired, his hectic flight slowing gradually to a canter, then a trot. At last he stopped, seemingly aware that the roller would not harm him, and turned to look at Bland. He dripped with sweat and his nostrils were distended and crimson-edged. The man spoke to him kindly: 'Well done, my son. It's not so bad, is it? Now we'll just try it again. Walk on.' And he flicked the whip gently at the horse's sodden hindquarters.

Gamecourt did a round or two more on the lunge quietly enough, but a further two days of lungeing in the roller were needed before he had accepted it completely and would allow the girth strap to be tightened. He was then introduced to a lightweight saddle, which he wore at exercise in place of the roller.

The next step in the colts' education was lungeing on two reins from the headcollar, one running from the far side round the hindquarters so that control of the head could be maintained from two sides and the animals taught to turn and lunge the other way. Then both reins were attached to the bit only and the colts were driven about from behind, in the way that a horse is driven from a cart. This part of the training is called long-reining and it is at this stage that mouths begin to form on yearlings, meaning that they learn to become responsive and sensitive to the bridle. To make sure that they were quiet enough to drive they were lunged each day beforehand until they were tired.

At this stage, if well-behaved enough, they were introduced

to the starting stalls. Most flat courses use iron stalls to ensure an even start (National Hunt races are longer, and a length gained or lost at the start is not so vital). The stalls are in one unit and can be towed about, depending upon where the race is to start from. Narrow parallel compartments contain the racehorses, who are led into the stalls from behind and shut in with a bar to stop them backing out again. When they are all in, the Starter presses a button, the gates in front of the horses fly open simultaneously, and the horses jump forward and race. An extra benefit to the level start is that horses are led in separately and so cannot kick one another, which quite often happens when a bunch of excited horses is lined up behind a tape start.

In the early days of starting stalls many horses on the race-course were frightened by their odd appearance and would refuse to go into them. Horses which could not be cajoled into the stalls were, and are, disqualified from the race. At Stanley House, as at most other racing stables, a set of stalls is kept on the premises and the horses are taught to use them right from the beginning. The quieter yearlings are long-reined into the stalls, the gates are closed in front of them and they are given a handful of grass and a pat. Then the gates are opened and they are walked on through. The more obstreperous youngsters are taught as soon as they are being ridden, and the lesson is repeated once a week throughout their first winter of training.

III

In many racing stables staff shortages cause the initial breaking-in period to be hurried, which means that yearlings

Bernard van Cutsem with
Maureen Foley at
Longchamp, 1968

Lord Derby (right) with
members of the Royal
Family at the Derby, 1966

Mountain Call's first crop at Woodlands, April 1971

Weanlings in a walled paddock at Knowsley

Long-reining the yearlings at Stanley House

Stan Warren gives Maureen Foley a leg up onto She Wolf outside her box
at Stanley House

At exercise on the Maples. She Wolf (Maureen Foley) leads from Bikini (Alan Woods),
with Indolent partly obscured

(*left*) Horses starting up
Bury Hill, Newmarket

(*bottom left*) Exercise on
Long Hill, Newmarket. In the
background a ploughed gallop
(the dark strip) cuts through
the turf

(*right*) Alcide and Dick Nicholls
in the stallion paddock at
Woodlands

(*below*) The blind mare
Samanda at Woodlands

She Wolf in her box at Stanley House

Indoor exercise in the covered school at Stanley House. Indolent leads from She Wolf and Bikini (rear horse unknown)

Brood mares in the paddock at Knowsley, autumn 1967. Sunsuit faces camera, Colin Dive in background

The house at Knowsley Park

Mick Ryan

Boxing up Mountain Call
for a race. Stan Warren
(in smock at left) stands
ready to push the horse in
from behind

Stan Warren

Bikini, ridden by
apprentice Alan Woods, in
the covered exercise school

Gamecourt, with his split pastern, is confined to his box. The grille on the top half of the door discourages unnecessary movement

Sweeping up after morning exercise, Ray Coppola (left), Maureen Foley (second from right)

Mountain Call at stud at Woodlands

Laureate at stud in South Africa

(*above*) Indolent cantering home to win the Hermitage Green Stakes at Haydock Park, September 5th, 1968, ridden by Willie Carson

(*top right*) Indolent, Willie Carson up, after winning the Prix des Aigles at Longchamp, October 13th, 1968, led by George Douglas and Michael Ryan (in hat)

(*bottom right*) Laureate winning the Lingfield Derby Trial, May 17th, 1968, ridden by Willie Carson

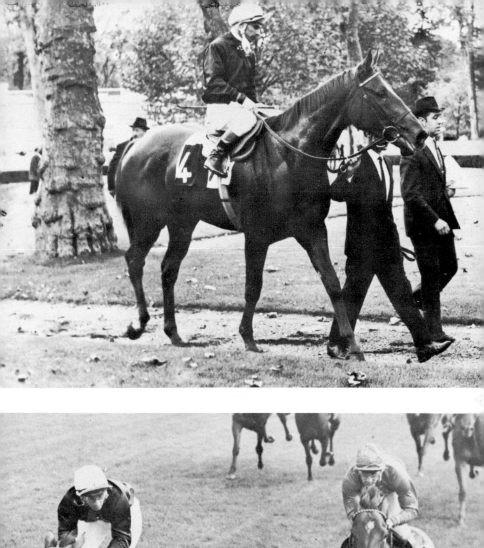

Laureate and Russ Maddock are led in by Tony Leaman after winning the Union Jack Stakes at Liverpool, March 28th, 1968; Michael Ryan is on the right

are being ridden within a week of their arrival in the yards. At Stanley House, which is comparatively well-staffed, yearlings are 'backed' (taught to accept a man's weight on their backs) about two weeks after they have come in. It is a three-man job, because the instincts that make a young horse reject a roller also warn him strongly against having something alive sitting on his back. One man holds the yearling's head while another is on hand to help the rider, who begins by leaning against the horse, and then very quietly lies across the horse's back.

Yearlings are usually backed in the loosebox, where they can be controlled more easily. It takes them about four days to get used to it: on the first two the rider merely lies across the animal's back, on the third the horse is asked to walk around the box, and on the fourth he is backed in the box and led out into the yard. On each day the yearling is first lunged and driven until he is quiet.

Laureate took the new sensation with indifference, though his muscles tensed when he was asked to move forward a few paces and the odd feeling of something alive on his back became more noticeable. Gamecourt, on the other hand, went rigid with fright when backed, and shot forward in nervous plunges when Bland, who was at his head, first asked him to move. The third man hung on to the rider's legs and the rider hung on to the roller. Gamecourt could just glimpse out of the corner of his eye the shape of a man lying above and behind his neck, and it took some time to reassure him.

When the colts had accepted their riders' presence and could be led about with someone lying across them, they were mounted properly and lunged with a man in the saddle. Quickly they learned to take orders from the saddle as the association between voice signals and hand and leg signals was made. They worked on their own in the paddocks until, when a dozen or so were in the same stage of learning, they were all loosed together, riders on board, to follow in a bunch behind a hack. The hack is a quiet old horse who can be depended upon to set a good example to the yearlings.

After two weeks of getting used to their new hard-food diet the colts' corn ration was increased to twelve pounds a day. They were working harder and needed the extra protein. From walking behind the hack they soon progressed to trotting in figures of eight, which taught them to answer the reins and the pressures of their riders' legs and to become accustomed to the shifting weight of the men in their saddles. Some needed more work circling to the right or to the left, since horses, like humans, are usually not born ambidextrous and will find it easier to bend one way rather than another. Gamecourt, for instance, was one-sided to the left and preferred to make left-handed turns. Unless taught to be more fluid to the right, he would find himself in trouble if asked to race on a right-handed course. A few horses are so markedly right- or left-sided that they can never run in races where the curve of the track is against them. The Derby, considered the greatest test on the flat, contains both right and left bends (though the right-handed curve is very gentle). It also requires the runners to race equally well up and down hill, which many horses cannot easily manage.

October came in with unsettled weather and a drop in the temperature. In the wet, windy mornings or afternoons, depending upon when there were men available to ride them, the yearlings followed the hack round the Maples, a circular half-mile of grass on the Stanley House estate. The leaves round the tree-lined edge of the track deepened and, on frosty mornings, were etched with white. Laureate and Gamecourt progressed from trotting to cantering.

On October 7th Lord Derby's fillies arrived from Knowsley and were stabled in the Sefton Yard to begin the breaking-in process. Indolent's behaviour was unremarkable, but She Wolf proved to be nervous and tricky to break. Bikini was so fond of people and so quiet that she was being ridden within a week of her arrival.

On the evening of the fifteenth Mountain Call arrived from Tattersalls's by horsebox and was added to the swelling number of yearlings in the Sefton Yard. Unlike Lord Derby's yearlings, he was not classically bred; his blood lines were those of a sprinter, and he already had the compact build that indicates a good one. His rich feeding for the yearling sales had lined his stomach with surplus fat and he had to be broken in more slowly than Derby's yearlings because his wind and insides were not so clean. His diet was immediately cut to the eight pounds of corn a day that the other unbroken yearlings were fed, but he got as much hay as he could eat and so was reasonably happy. Because of his extensive early training he was much quieter in the stable than the others and was thoroughly used to being tied up while his coat was groomed and his bedding changed and shaken up. Since the men could not know if other yearlings had had these lessons, the general rule was that all new arrivals should be tied up for stable handling with a piece of string, which would snap easily if they ran backwards and save them the fright of finding their heads tied. Mountain Call never tested the strength of his string.

Having already been taught to lunge, Mountain Call's first

lessons were a mere formality. He had had so much previous handling that he was backed and ridden at the end of his first week. However, his progress to trotting and cantering had to be taken very slowly to allow time for some of the fat to come off him.

IV

Bernard van Cutsem, the British-born son of a Dutch count, is a tall, thin man with great charm and presence. His discipline in his stable yard is absolute.

As a young man, van Cutsem took a general degree at Cambridge University. The 1930s saw the last of the great days of Cambridge in which sporting interests were an acceptable substitute for academic work. Van Cutsem worked hard during his three University years; but not at studying. 'I'm sorry to say that the whole time I was at Cambridge I only went to one lecture. I can't remember what it was about,' he said. 'After that there was too much to do.'

As an undergraduate, van Cutsem had four main horse interests: organizing the hunter trials which were a regular autumn feature, training and racing his point-to-pointers (he rode his own horses to win eight or nine of these races), organizing the University's point-to-point meeting at Cottenham in the spring, and running the University Drag.

The Cambridge University Drag is an amateur hunt without a quarry. The scent is laid by a runner, dragging behind him a sock soaked in fox's urine, which is bought from London Zoo. Because the scent is very fresh (the runner gets only a half-hour start), and because the line is worked out in advance and the fences have been (supposedly) examined beforehand for safety, the pace is much faster than a foxhunt and the hunt has more of the character of an old-fashioned steeplechase. Often the undergraduate who chooses the line thinks more of his reputation than his neck, so some of the obstacles are enormous and would, in cold blood, be unthinkable. Meets were, and are, often held at country houses where the hosts are generous with their drink. Otherwise a visit to a pub on the way to a Drag meet is imperative.

The great days of the Cambridge Drag are past – the days when an undergraduate would take eight or nine hunters up to University with him; when the country was not fouled by wire and large tracts of land belonged to owner-enthusiasts who co-operated by setting up formidable fences to jump; when van Cutsem, as Whip, and, in his last year, as Master, hunted twenty couple of Welsh bitches (the best kind of foxhounds). Nowadays the University Drag mostly has to make do with six or seven couple of reject hounds, thrown out by foxhunts all over the country. There are not so many big landowners about, and the Drag often has to travel for two or three hours to find someone who owns enough land to make it possible to lay a line of decent length.

But the courage and enthusiasm endure. Two fairly recent instances will illustrate the point. In 1968, on a filthy February day with a high wind and heavy sleet, an undergraduate who had never jumped a fence before took forty-eight fences on an eight-mile point. He fell off forty-eight times. He has since become Master of his own Drag pack, using bloodhounds, which have better noses than foxhounds.

And in the spring of 1971, the Cambridge Drag jumped round the horrifying Burghley Park Cross-Country Course *backwards*, most mounted on hired riding-stable plugs. This was not, in fact, intentional – the runner started off the wrong way by mistake.

Van Cutsem graduated from Cambridge in 1938 with no doubts about what his career would be. He went into racing immediately. Though he had no previous experience other than training his own point-to-pointers, he applied for, and got, a licence to train his own horses both on the flat and under National Hunt rules. He set himself up at Exning, the village near Newmarket where he lives today, and was almost at once confounded by the outbreak of war.

Van Cutsem served as an officer in the Life Guards during World War II, and did not come back into racing until 1955. Then he set up again at Newmarket, and in 1963 moved to his present training yard, Stanley House Stables. Though van Cutsem's Cambridge record shows that he is a brilliant horseman, he was initially looked on by the racing fraternity as a bit of a dilettante, but his winning record soon showed that he was entirely serious. He has a gift for running the right horse in the right race – a paramount quality in a trainer, whose job, having brought a horse to the peak of fitness, is to enter it in races against horses that it is likely to beat. He has become one of the most brilliant men in racing.

None but the highly dedicated would take up the life of a racehorse trainer. It is a life of worry and of very hard work. The worry stems from having responsibility for sometimes as much as a million pounds' worth of other people's horseflesh, which is overly subject to accident. (How can he say to an owner, 'Your £15,000 filly dropped young Jones on the Heath this morning and ran off and got hit by a car. I *am* sorry.'?) The hard work is roughly this: in the summer months van Cutsem must be at the stables by seven fifteen in the morning to look his horses over as they come out for exercise and to hear news from his head lad about their health – one may be coughing, another off its feed, a third have a bit of heat in its leg. Then he drives out to the training grounds, giving instructions for the distance each horse should gallop and the speed at which it should go. Differences in temperament and constitution mean that no two horses can be assumed to need the same amount of work. After he has seen the first lot work, he has breakfast and is back in time to watch the second lot turn out for exercise. Sometimes, if he has a runner at a distant meeting, he doesn't have time to watch the second lot work, and so the horses that have races imminent are sent out with the first lot.

After morning stables, if it is a race day, he goes by car or light aircraft to the race meeting, arriving in time to saddle the horse and to give instructions to the jockey. In the Paddock he may also meet the owner of the horse, with whom he goes over the animal's probable performance, and, later, its actual performance. Time spent at the races, apart from what he can learn from watching his own horses run, is invaluable to van Cutsem because it gives him the opportunity of studying the form of other people's horses against which he may later have to decide whether or not to match his own. After racing he dashes home in time for evening stables, where he looks over every horse in his charge and feels its legs for heat.

This routine takes up much of his six-day week, but there is also a great deal of paperwork to be done. Corn, hay, and straw must be chosen and paid for; veterinary and farriers' bills debited to the right horse so that owners' accounts can be made up fairly; entries made long in advance and the

forfeit stages noted; horseboxes organized and accommodation reserved for horses and lads who will stay overnight at
the races. There are also written reports on the progress of
horses to be made up and sent out, and a generous time
allowance has to be made for telephone calls and for time
spent socially with owners, many of whom are personal
friends. Not surprisingly, van Cutsem needs the services of
two secretaries to keep him up-to-date.

Most important, although this is not officially part of his
job, a trainer's knowledge of form has also to be used for the
placing of well-judged bets. (Profits from training racehorses,
except those who win valuable prizes, are minimal to non-
existent. Since only one out of four horses ever wins a race of
any sort, trainers with small stables – van Cutsem is not one
of these – must rely on betting if they are to expect any
financial reward.)

As the flat season draws to a close and horses begin to leave
the main Stanley House yard to go to stud or to be sold,
yearlings who have been broken in are gradually brought
up from the Sefton Yard to replace them. Because stable
hands get two-and-a-half per cent of the prize money when
the horses that they 'do' win races, and on the principle that
they work better with horses that they like, van Cutsem
usually allows his lads to choose their yearlings for themselves.
Two exceptions in the 1966 batch of yearlings were Laureate,
whom van Cutsem assigned to Matty McCormack, an experienced and sympathetic handler of Aureole colts, and the
nervous and tricky She Wolf, whom he gave to his most
trusted stable girl, Maureen Foley.

The yearlings soon settled in to the regular work routine
of the main yard. The working day began at six forty-five,

when the lads arrived in the yard. Each lad had two horses to look after. They cleaned out the stables of their first horses, saddled up and were off to the gallops by seven thirty. At nine o'clock they returned to the stable yard, unsaddled and cleaned off their horses and replaced their rugs. Then they shook down fresh bedding, cleaned out the water mangers and fetched more hay. Stan Warren apportioned the breakfast feeds, which the lads fed to the horses before going off for their own breakfasts at about half past nine. Minor veterinary dressings were done at this time by Warren or by Michael Ryan, the travelling head lad (Ryan, Mick Ryan's son, was the man in charge of horses while they were away racing). The damage done at exercise was hardly ever serious, but nearly every day at least one of the horses would have scratched or knocked itself while working, and there were always some who needed support bandages for their legs.

The lads came back from breakfast at ten and mucked out their second lot. These horses went out at ten thirty for an hour-and-a-quarter's exercise, and were usually 'done up' and fed by twelve fifteen. The lads swept up and tidied the stable yard before they went for lunch.

Evening stables began at four thirty, when the lads returned to 'dress over their two'. Dirty bedding was removed, and piled on the muck heap, from which it would later be carted away for mushroom cultivation. The horses were very thoroughly groomed, given fresh hay and water and, lastly, their evening feeds. Unless he was away at a distant race meeting, van Cutsem would arrive at about five thirty and have the rugs off every horse in the stables (except in very cold weather) for a personal inspection. If he found anything unsatisfactory he would tell Warren, who would pass it on to the appropriate lad; similarly, if the lad had any comment to make about his horse he would tell the head lad, who would pass it on to the trainer in their daily discussions. Evening stables was usually finished by six thirty.

The winter routine differed from the normal work routine in that the first lot could not go out for exercise until dawn, which in mid-winter comes later than seven thirty, and in that the exercise periods were shorter. With the flat season ended, the horses did not need to be racing fit but simply in good health. This was maintained by walking and trotting with a couple of gentle canters thrown in to keep their muscles going.

When the yearlings first came into the main yard they usually formed a third lot under the tutelage of a quiet old hack. Some of the lads found themselves with three horses to do, a seasonal dilemma caused by the arrival of new animals before all the cast-offs had left. By this time – early November – all the yearlings could at least be ridden at a trot, and the more advanced, which included Laureate and Gamecourt but not the fillies or Mountain Call, at a canter. Warren thought of them as babies and treated them as such. 'You have to be very patient with them,' he said. 'They've no idea of how to move with a man on their backs.'

Potential early two-year-old runners, those who on growth and breeding might be ready to race in the spring of 1967, were put into the warmest stables to bring them on faster. In the late autumn of 1966 Laureate, She Wolf and Mountain Call looked promising enough to qualify for special attention. Gamecourt was also given one of the warmer boxes, but this was because of his health. He had grown into a narrow, fragile-looking yearling with a thin neck and a delicate look

about him. Bikini and Indolent were not given special treatment, because they would almost certainly come to their full
strength late. They were 'backward' – overgrown and rangy,
with the potential weakness of children who, looking older
than others of the same age, are actually more easily fatigued
than their contemporaries because of having put so much
energy into growing.

By mid-November all of the yearlings had been brought up
to the main yard and were doing regular work. They became
easily overheated in their shaggy winter coats, not yet thinned
down with grooming or sleekened from the habitual wearing
of rugs, and would sweat in sticky patches round the shoulders
and in the sockets at the tops of their legs. To prevent this they
were trace-clipped: their coats were shaved to the skin in the
places that were most likely to sweat, but their heads, backs,
and legs were left covered.

The trace-clipping was done in the afternoons, in a bare-
floored loosebox so that the clipped-off coat could be swept up.
The yearlings' coats were clipped against the grain with
electric clippers, and two or three runs with the clippers were
needed to get the hair down really short. She Wolf and
Indolent, who were ticklish round the flanks, had to have
twitches put on their upper lips while their backsides were
shaved. Mountain Call was ticklish under the belly and got the
same treatment. Bikini, bored, rested a hind leg throughout,
which put her hindquarters out of alignment and made it hard
for Warren, who was using the clippers, to get the straight
lines of clipping to balance on each side. Each yearling took
about an hour to clip. The older horses were also trace-clipped
in winter.

When the clipping was done, each yearling was given a

blanket to wear when in the stable. It buckled in front across the shoulders and was kept in place by a surcingle girthed round the middle, and by a strap under the belly and another round the flanks. Thus secured it could reasonably be expected to stay on, but Bikini found it irksome and managed on most nights to get rid of it. She learned somehow to get it off over her head with all the straps still fastened and would often trample it into her bedding.

December proved mostly wet and cold. Horses retiring from the season before had left the yard by then, and the yearlings formed the bulk of the second lot. In the intervals of milder weather they worked in bunches, cantering three or four abreast to teach them to gallop with others. But ground conditions limited winter cantering, and on frosty mornings, when fast work would have jarred their brittle legs, the yearlings walked and trotted about. With the inattention and imbalance of extreme youth they tended to place their feet carelessly and their riders had always to be alert to check tripping and stumbling. Childish bogeys – a falling leaf, or a bird flying suddenly out of a hedge – would send a yearling spinning away, more often than not upsetting his companions. Sometimes the provocation would come from inside the horse's head, an imagined attacker or sudden playfulness that would give the rider no warning at all. Mountain Call and Laureate were particularly wilful – both of them were headstrong, and they were often deliberately naughty. Bikini, by contrast, was so quiet that a child could have ridden her.

On Christmas Day, a Sunday, the first snow fell. Most of the horses stayed indoors because of the holiday, but a few of the older colts went out for a twenty-minute walk and trot. Van Cutsem had saved five per cent of the total stakes won by the horses during the year as a Christmas present for his lads, and divided it equally according to whether or not each had worked the full season. It was a generous present. Despite the celebration it caused, nearly everyone turned up for work during the holiday to save someone else from having to do his job.

The year ended in cloud and rain. Mountain Call, whose greed was so great that he could not be stopped from eating his straw, was bedded on peat moss.

1967

Winter

DURING the first half of January, cold weather kept the horses off the gallops. When it was not actually too hard to canter, the thawing ground was usually too slippery to be useable. Most of the Newmarket horses exercised on the roads in the worst of the weather, but Stanley House Stables had a circular covered school, one furlong (one-eighth of a mile) round, which was used for exercise when there was frost, snow or rain. Van Cutsem saw no point in getting the horses wet or cold if it could be avoided. Though they were dry and out of the cutting wind in the exercise school, it was still very cold. The lads wore the thickest clothing they had, but nothing could properly protect their feet. For them the worst part of winter work was the dismounting drop at the end of exercise onto feet that felt as if they would shatter on contact with the ground.

Indoor exercise was dull. The two-year-olds – the yearlings of December – did three trotting sessions, each four times round the school, with walking periods in between. The older horses did four trots of four times round. It was boring work both for the horses and for the stable lads. While the indoor work period lasted Stan Warren heard more complaints from the lads than he did during all the other months of the year combined.

'Stable lad' is racing jargon for groom and has nothing to do with age: lads at Newmarket vary from fifteen to seventy. Most of van Cutsem's lads live on the Stanley House premises, the apprentices and some of the single lads in the hostel which is the west wing of the main stable block, and the married lads in cottages on the estate.

Every young man who apprentices himself to a racing stable does so because he hopes to become a jockey. Most start their apprenticeship at fifteen, the minimum school leaving age. Many have never been on a horse before and have to be taught to ride on a pony or on a quiet old hack. Usually these tiny young men know nothing about racing, and the stable to which they become apprenticed is chosen arbitrarily, through an advertisement in a newspaper, or a relative who knows a man who knows a trainer. The apprenticeship lasts five years, during which the lad gets full board and lodging and a small cash allowance. If it becomes apparent in the early stages that he does not get on with horses he is allowed to break his contract, but otherwise he is at his master's disposal for up to fifty weeks of the year. He cannot transfer to another stable without his master's consent; nor, if he proves good enough to be a jockey, can he race for anyone other than his master without special permission.

Having spent much of their early lives wishing they were as tall and heavy as their contemporaries, apprentices spend the second half of their teens worrying that they may grow too big to be jockeys. Many of them do — even the most successful flat-race jockey cannot afford to weigh much more than 112 pounds — and these overweights, provided they are not unreasonably heavy, stay on in the stables as lads or occasionally graduate to National Hunt racing, where the weight allowances are greater. Most apprentices never become jockeys at all, and only the most intelligent have a hope of being top jockeys. A good jockey must have brains, courage,

and quick reactions. Being a good horseman is not in itself
enough, and very occasionally a man may become a successful
jockey without being much of a horseman.

Quite a few of the stable 'lads' in Newmarket are in fact
women. These girls, who have not the slightest chance of
making fortunes – the British ruling, quite unfairly, does not
allow women to race professionally – nevertheless work the
same long, hard hours in the stables as the lads because of their
love for horses. Some trainers prefer to employ girls rather
than lads because they feel that women have more patience
with horses and they like staff to be motivated by the pleasure
of doing the job.

Maureen Foley, who looked after She Wolf, was described
by Bernard van Cutsem as 'the best stable girl I've ever had'.
Always fond of horses, she started her working life with them
by studying for and passing the difficult British Horse
Society's Instructors' Examination, the equivalent of the
British Cavalry Instructors' qualification. She then got a job
with show jumpers and cared for as many as nine horses a
day in return for board and keep plus £3 a week. On her own
account, after this she found looking after only two racehorses
almost a holiday, and was staggered to discover that she
would earn £20 a week for the job.

She Wolf was a strong-minded filly who liked to show her
authority in the stable. If a visitor came into her box she
would lay back her ears and sidle over to him as if trying to
push him out. Stan Warren thought her a bit mean, but
Maureen found that once she had shown that she would pay
no attention to this threatening behaviour, the filly was very
affectionate. She began to enjoy looking after She Wolf,
taking pride in her improving manners and appearance.

Since the weather was cold, Maureen groomed without completely removing She Wolf's rug. She turned the rug forward and brushed the nearside hindquarters and then the offside and the tail, and while at it also brushed the rug free of loose hairs. Then she turned the rug back over the clean hindquarters and did the front and middle part of the filly. She Wolf was ticklish under the belly and around the flanks, and Maureen had to be careful not to get kicked when she cleaned these parts. Then, with the rug replaced, she did the neck and mane. All this happened with She Wolf tied up to a ring on the wall so that Maureen could come and go outside to get the various bits of grooming equipment without fear of She Wolf's getting loose. When the filly's body was finished to her satisfaction, Maureen closed the door of the box, took off the headcollar, and brushed over She Wolf's face. Before going out in the morning and again during evening grooming, Maureen cleaned out She Wolf's eyes, nose, mouth, and dock with a damp sponge, and cleaned her feet free of mud and dung with a hoofpick. Picking out the feet before morning exercise was done mainly to check that the filly's shoes were in position.

Coming in from exercise on muddy mornings Maureen washed She Wolf's feet in a bucket of water and dried them carefully with a piece of sacking, paying special attention to the heels, which could crack open if left to dry out, much as a human's hands get chapped in cold weather. As the days passed, a fine sheen began to show on She Wolf's coat as Maureen repeatedly sponged her over (this was done after morning exercise to get rid of the sweat), rubbed her dry with the saddle rubber, and then polished her with a brush.

In mid-January the weather cleared. Icicles that had hung

from the eaves of the exercise school began to drip and then to run water, and the days turned sunny and mild. The horses were able to go back to work on the Heath. The lads began again to joke with each other, and the horses frisked and bucked all over the place with pleasure. The young two-year-olds resumed their cantering lessons, gradually learning to work in single file like proper racehorses.

Soon after she started cantering, She Wolf developed windgalls on her hind legs. These puffy swellings just above her fetlock joints came on because her legs were not really strong enough for galloping. Maureen put the thick bandages called Newmarket Cloths on her hind legs for support; but even so it was apparent that She Wolf, who was big and overgrown, was still too backward to do serious work as a racehorse. The same was true of Indolent and Bikini: Indolent was rangy and Bikini had become a big, affectionate baby. Bernard van Cutsem thought the fillies needed time to grow up.

'I didn't think they could be trained as two-year-olds,' he said. 'They weren't forward enough for racing. It seemed pointless to keep them in training. It might even be worse than pointless because they could pick up bad habits on the Heath.

'I thought they would be safer out. They would have the spring grass through, and then the sun. They would develop more.'

Near the end of February, in fine weather, dry and mild, he had She Wolf, Indolent, and Bikini turned away at Woodlands for the spring, to play about in a paddock once again under the benevolent eye of Mick Ryan.

II

Lord Derby's two-year-olds were bred for the classics, for the five greatest three-year-old races of the English season. The announcements for the 1968 classics came out in the *Racing Calendar* early in 1967. The Two Thousand Guineas (one mile; colts only) was scheduled for May 1st; the One Thousand Guineas (one mile; fillies only) for May 2nd; the Derby (one mile, four furlongs; both sexes) for May 29th; the Oaks (one mile, four furlongs; fillies only) for May 31st; the St Leger (one mile, six furlongs, 132 yards; mixed) for September 11th. Entries for the 1968 classics closed on February 22nd, 1967, and van Cutsem, like all other trainers with classic hopes, had to make decisions at a time when his horses were far too young for their abilities to be even guessed at.

'You're completely in the dark,' he said. 'You've got to put in the classics anything that has the breeding and is a good individual. It's an appalling lottery.'

Van Cutsem felt that the fillies and Laureate were entitled on breeding to be entered in all the classics. Gamecourt, who was by a staying stallion, he thought unlikely to be a miler, and so he left him out of the Guineas. The entries he sent off, at an initial total cost of £300, to Messrs Weatherby, the agents of the Jockey Club, were:

Laureate for the Two Thousand Guineas;
Bikini, Indolent, and She Wolf for the One Thousand Guineas;
Laureate and Gamecourt for the Derby (fillies, though eligible, are not normally as strong as colts, and only six have ever won a Derby);

Bikini, Indolent, and She Wolf for the Oaks;
Bikini, Indolent, She Wolf, Laureate, and Gamecourt for
the St Leger.

The value of the classic races is explained by the cost of the
entries and the peculiar timing of them. In the 1968 Derby,
for example, 590 horses were entered in the spring of their
two-year-old year. In the next fifteen months there were three
forfeit stages, and a declaration to run, upon which yet another
fee became due, four days before the race. At each stage a
horse could be taken out, but its accumulated entry money
would be held to swell the Derby prize. Added money helps to
make the Derby the richest of the English three-year-old
races, though the prize is insignificant when compared with the
fat purses available in French and American racing. The precise amount of the Derby cannot, because of the forfeits, be
known until shortly before the race.

Mountain Call, who was sprint-bred, had no classic engage-
ments.

III

March came in with showers and sunny periods, though there
were frosts at night. On most mornings the ground was soft
enough to allow the horses to canter, and van Cutsem began
to get an idea of the potential of the two-year-olds. They were
behind the three-year-olds in progress. 'It's very much a
climatic thing in this country,' he explained. 'The two-year-
olds come when the weather comes. The older horses are
always much more consistent.'

Laureate was being brought on gently, saved as a possible

classic prospect, and Gamecourt was still not a hundred per cent right, but Mountain Call was shaping up into a well-advanced colt. Van Cutsem thought he was developing fast enough to be a likely early runner. 'Mountain Call *looks* like a two-year-old,' the trainer said, admiring his colt's sturdy, muscular body and glossy hide. In comparison, Laureate and Gamecourt looked leggy and fragile.

With the flat season approaching, the stable jockeys began to turn up for exercise to get the feel of the horses and to get themselves fit. Russ Maddock, an Australian who was first jockey to van Cutsem, turned up twice a week to try out the new horses. He 'rode work' on all of them; whenever one was being tested at a gallop, Maddock was on its back. The stretched-out feel, differing in each horse in its length of stride and readiness to try, was invaluable to the man who would later ride them in races. The veteran Doug Smith, Lord Derby's first jockey, who was starting his last season before retiring to train, also came and rode. So did Willie Carson, who had been engaged as second jockey to Lord Derby and was to take over from Smith the following year.

The two-year-olds worked mainly on Lord Derby's private gallops, which run alongside the railway track that goes from Newmarket to Bury St Edmunds. It was here that Maddock rode work on Mountain Call for the first time. One of the many things that Stan Warren, as head lad the man responsible for the horses in van Cutsem's absence, had to keep in his head was the railway timetable, because a passing train would upset the racehorses. On the morning when Maddock first rode Mountain Call, Warren misjudged the times. Just as the string was approaching the gallops a train came by. It would have been difficult enough if it had kept reasonably quiet, but as it passed the horses, only thirty or forty yards away, it whistled. Mountain Call reacted fast, ducking out from under Maddock, who was catapulted off but managed to keep his hold on the reins. Afterwards, Warren was very apologetic.

When they came back into the stable yard, Maddock nursing a bruise on his left thigh, Arthur Bell, a strong lad who had once or twice exercised Mountain Call, came out to meet them. He had been watching Mountain Call for some time and had been impressed with him. Now he asked Maddock whether he should become the colt's regular lad. The Australian, who had thought the colt promising, advised Bell to take him on.

Mountain Call was normally quiet to ride, even lazy, but going into the gallops he nearly always bucked and kicked out. Arthur Bell soon learned to be prepared for this; even so, he was sometimes unseated. Usually he managed to hold on to the reins, but occasionally Mountain Call would twist from his grasp and gallop off alone.

Loose horses are a major problem for a head lad. It is quite a common sight to see a horse galloping by itself down the Bury Road, since most of them make for the traffic control where they regularly cross on their way back to the stables. Every year two or three horses are killed on the Newmarket roads. Drivers passing through the town on the main road to the east coast are often unused to racehorses and sound their horns or rev up their engines, sometimes frightening a horse badly enough to make it panic and run into a car. Strangely enough, good racehorses who get loose and gallop home usually hurt themselves. The bad ones come home un-blemished, either because they are 'pigs' (lazy animals who are not likely to travel fast) or rogues, who always look ten yards ahead to see if they can find anything to fuss about.

When a horse gets loose Warren follows as quickly as possible on his pony, galloping towards the railed entrance to the gallops to stop the horse from getting through onto the road. Other head lads and trainers always help to catch a loose animal, but the lads on racehorses take no part because their mounts might get kicked.

Most loose horses are principally interested in getting home for food, but Mountain Call was different. He had big ideas about himself as a stallion and used to attack other horses whenever he got free, galloping around until he spotted a likely victim and then rearing up on his hind legs to have a bite at it.

He gave no sign of this coltish behaviour in the stables; at least not to Arthur Bell, who found him almost sloppily affectionate. He liked having his lips played with and had a habit of sticking out his tongue. It was only partly because Mountain Call liked the salty taste of his skin that Bell got licked and slobbered on. The colt was not so kind to the other lads and would sometimes take a nip at them. He had a highly-developed sense of territory and did not like intruders in his box.

Gamecourt, on the other hand, was thought by everyone to be one of the sweetest horses in the stable. He had no vices whatsoever and was such a kind ride that even the younger apprentices were allowed to ride him. His honesty and hard work on the gallops also contrasted with Mountain Call, who tailed off lazily and had to be pushed along by Bell.

Compared with Gamecourt, and indeed compared with just about anything in the stable, Laureate was wilfully difficult. His proud, masculine disposition frightened a lot of the lads and none of them was keen to go into his box alone, though

Matty McCormack found him 'not too troublesome'. As had always been the case, Laureate got extra attention and was always treated with respect. Like Mountain Call, he was a lazy worker. 'He doesn't do a stroke,' Warren said. But nonetheless he thought very highly of the horse, as did van Cutsem. Would Laureate, so well-bred and so high-couraged, grow up to be a Derby winner? He was certainly developing into one of the best classic prospects of the two-year-olds.

As March drew on and the beginning of the flat season approached, the horses who were likely to be early runners were put into full training. Van Cutsem did not want his horses strained unnecessarily by having to gallop with heavy riders, and so just before the season began he weighed all the lads on the stable scales. Anyone over 126 pounds was not allowed to work the horses at full speed.

Spring

THE British flat-racing season opened on March 25th. It was a cold week, and the wind drove the rain across Newmarket Heath. The horses exercised in blankets and nightcaps — hoods that covered the ears, making them look a bit like court jesters. Each afternoon the drying room was hung with sodden horse clothing.

Most of the two-year-olds went out in the second lot for an hour of walking and trotting with some light cantering thrown in, but the few who seemed likely to be early runners were getting a lot of steady work. Twice a week they were stretched out at full gallop, which gave van Cutsem an idea of their potential. Sometimes he matched them against older horses of known ability to help him pinpoint the possibilities of each youngster. Mostly he worked them with jockeys on board, to give them the best professional teaching. At first he galloped the two-year-olds over two furlongs, stopping them while they were still keen: then he stretched it out to three and four. Four-and-a-half would be the maximum distance before they were raced. Early two-year-old races are short and he would be able to see at the track whether they needed a longer distance.

Van Cutsem did not really believe in racing young horses, feeling that overstraining them early might cause permanent damage. 'In theory, I'd like not to run two-year-olds,' he said, 'but in practice it's impossible not to. I'm talking about nice two-year-olds; not little rats. But it's unfair to owners not to race them, especially if they turn out later to be no good.' Mountain Call, however, needed a race because he was big and fat and advanced. He was by a sprint stallion, and obviously had the strength, so van Cutsem entered him for the Stuntney Maiden Stakes, a mid-April race at Newmarket for two-year-old colts and geldings who had never won. No one expected much of the colt. Russ Maddock, who was to be his jockey, thought he 'wouldn't beat my hat in a gallop at home'. But horses who are idle at home are often stimulated by a change of scene, and Maddock kept an open mind.

Mountain Call had thus far shown no competitive spirit and always worked at half speed, which meant that the stable had no real idea about whether he was any good or not. He was so lazy that even the hack could beat him in a gallop. Nonetheless he was 'wound up' for the April 18th meeting. ' "Wound up" means tightened to the breaking point; tuned up,' explained Maddock. 'He feels as if he's walking on eggshells. He walks, but he's so light and keen that he doesn't touch the ground.'

By this time all of the two-year-olds were thoroughly used to the starting stalls. Two days before Mountain Call was to run for the first time he was put into the stalls with the gates closed in front of him and then asked by Maddock to jump out fast when they opened. He did this so well that it was not necessary to repeat the lesson.

On April 17th, the day before the race, Mountain Call had an easy day's work to make him fresh for the following day. That night Bell bedded him on wood shavings so that he would not be able to overeat.

On the morning of April 18th, which was sunny and cool with scattered white clouds in the sky, Mountain Call did not go out to work at all. He had his normal breakfast feed and was led out for a twenty-minute walk to loosen him up. Instead of taking another horse out to exercise on the second lot, Bell spent the time polishing up his golden coat and staying with him while the blacksmith changed the colt's work shoes, which weighed 28 ounces, to his first set of racing plates. These are made of aluminium and are very light – only 5½ ounces. They would probably be useless after the race, though they could last as long as a week if Mountain Call was kept off the roads. When the colt had been plated, Michael Ryan came in to plait up his mane. Shortly before midday Mountain Call's hay net and water bucket were removed. Horses cannot race on full stomachs.

After lunch, Arthur Bell reappeared, wearing a suit. The Stuntney Maiden Stakes, a five-furlong sprint, was the last of the six races of the day and was not due to start until four forty, so there was no particular hurry to get to the course. Mountain Call was boxed up and driven the short distance through the town to the Newmarket Rous Course (part of the Rowley Mile), where Bell walked him around a small paddock with the other runners until it was time to saddle up. Mountain Call's ears flicked back and forth at the strangeness of it all, but otherwise he was calm. Like all of the other runners in the race he was to carry 124 pounds, so he was tacked up with one of Maddock's heavier racing saddles. There were twenty-two entries for the race. One of them was Panpiper, Mountain Call's childhood companion, who was also making his first appearance on a track.

Half an hour before the race the runners were called into

the main paddock so that the crowd could have a look at them before placing their bets. Mountain Call, now saddled up, wore a blanket over his saddle to protect him against the April wind. Owners, trainers, and jockeys gathered in the middle of the paddock to discuss the way their horses should be ridden. Maddock, who had ridden in the preceding race on a horse trained by van Cutsem for F. W. Burmann, was a little late because of having had to change into Isaac Kornberg's silks. Kornberg's colours, freshly laundered by Maddock's valet, were lime green with an orange sash and a green cap with black spots.

Van Cutsem, usually very positive in his instructions, had nothing much to say to Maddock in the paddock because Mountain Call had no past form to go on. He had been so lazy at home that he had not even an elementary knowledge of competitive galloping, so everything he learned about racing would have to be taught on the racecourse.

The request 'Jockeys get mounted, please' came over the loudspeaker. Bell brought Mountain Call over to van Cutsem and Maddock. Michael Ryan was there, too, in his capacity as travelling head lad, and he helped Bell to strip off Mountain Call's rug and tighten the girths. Mountain Call showed no excitement and was not in the least alarmed by his new surroundings or by the crowd, who were hurrying away to place their bets. The favourite, according to the flashing lights above the Totalizator, was a colt called Czar Alexander, also one who had never run before. Mountain Call's chances were rated at 100–6 and Panpiper was slightly more fancied at 100–7.

Ryan gave Maddock a leg up and Bell led them out onto the course. He unclipped the lead-rein and let the colt go to canter down to the start of the five-furlong straight. Mountain Call was still very cool. He went down to the post at a lazy pace to join the bunch of excited young horses who were walking about behind the starting stalls. Loading up the twenty-two maidens took some time because several of them played up and would not go into the stalls. The worst of these had to be blindfolded and pushed in from behind by the horse handlers who are always present to get difficult horses loaded up. Mountain Call walked easily into his stall at the first time of asking.

When all the runners were in, the white flag went up and the announcement 'Under Starter's Orders' was made. Maddock gathered Mountain Call under him and tried to prepare him to jump out fast when the gates opened.

The Starter's hand came down on the button and the gates flew open. Mountain Call struck out fast and for the first time in his life really galloped. The flood of charging two-year-olds seemed to exhilarate him and at the first furlong post he was in front, pulling hard on the reins. At the second post he was still there, showing a promising turn of foot, but either his strength or his enthusiasm did not last and he was overtaken by several of his competitors. The race ended in a battle between Czar Alexander and a colt called Love's Violin, with Czar Alexander holding on by three-quarters of a length in a time of 1 minute 1.84 seconds, nothing exceptional. Mountain Call finished ninth, ahead of Panpiper. Maddock pulled him up and trotted him back to the paddock entrance, where Arthur Bell was waiting to lead him in. Bell looked inquiringly at Maddock. 'All right' was all that Maddock said.

They went into the general unsaddling area, where Maddock

dismounted and took off his saddle. He stopped to talk to Bernard van Cutsem, who had walked over to look at the colt. The jockey's opinion of a horse is of great value to the trainer. 'He's a complete baby,' Maddock said, 'but I think he'll improve.' Michael Ryan came up with a bucket of horse shampoo, and he and Bell washed Mountain Call carefully all over, except for the head, legs, and hindquarters, to get rid of the thick sweat. The water contained a mild disinfectant, because it was just possible that Maddock's saddle might have been used on a horse that had an infection such as ringworm. Mountain Call was so hot that he steamed heavily through the shampoo. When he was thoroughly sponged down Ryan scraped off the shampoo with a thin piece of hard rubber, which removed most of the moisture from his coat. Bell put a cooler over him — a rug of light fabric that looked like a string vest — and led him around to dry. When he had stopped blowing he was allowed half a bucketful of tepid* water, which he drank thirstily, and when he was completely dry and relaxed the damp cooler was taken away and his rugs were put on. Then he was led back into the horsebox for the short journey home.

Back at the stable yard Mountain Call was fed a warm mash and plenty of hay. He was left to sleep it off overnight, and the following day, since he had worked so hard the day before, Bell led him out for a walk to ease his tired muscles, and allowed him to pick grass. His belly was tucked up and he had lost a bit of weight, but this was to be expected.

'I wasn't *over*-pleased with Mountain Call that time,' Maddock said afterwards. 'I was just satisfied. He had showed

* This is usually called 'chilled' water by racing people, meaning that the chill has been taken off with the addition of some hot water.

speed in the early stages of the race, which is the first thing you look for in a two-year-old. When you know they have the speed, then you can begin to put the stamina into them.'

Stanley House Stables were a little the wiser about Mountain Call. The official Form Book (a weekly commentary on horses who have raced, written by the staff of the *Sporting Chronicle*) summed him up in one word: 'Backward.'

II

Mountain Call's next race was on May 3rd at Newmarket over the same five-furlong straight. The going was good and the day dry and cold. This time Mountain Call brought Kornberg's lime-green-and-orange colours past the finishing post fifteenth of the seventeen runners. Love's Violin, promoted favourite on his last showing, again finished second. The race was the May Maiden Stakes, and Mountain Call was reported by the Form Book to have shown 'Early speed' – a public step up from 'Backward', but something that van Cutsem and Maddock already knew from his first race.

Mountain Call's experiences in racing made no difference to his behaviour at home. He was as lazy as ever and still made no effort on the gallops. Sometimes he would bound along for two furlongs or so, but always he would pack it in. He seemed to have no competitive spirit.

His next run was in the Parth Maiden Stakes at Kempton Park, just south of London, on May 27th. It was another five-furlong race, at a very good track which attracts first-class horses. On the afternoon of May 26th, since the racecourse was some distance from Newmarket, he was boxed up and driven to the meeting to stay overnight in the Kempton racing stables. Arthur Bell went with him. The preceding few days had been sunny with heavy showers, and the going on the Kempton course was heavy. Mountain Call came out of the starting stalls fast and settled down to show what he could do.

He could, it turned out, do a lot: he ran like a champion, straight and true, refusing to give an inch. The race was a close thing between him, Loveridge and Last Shoe, a colt who had already won two races and was penalized ten pounds for having done so. The three leaders were so close together at the winning post that it was a photo-finish for all three places. The photograph showed Loveridge as the winner, with Last Shoe second and Mountain Call third. The distances between them were a head and a short head (a short head is the minimum winning or losing margin in a race). Mountain Call had finished four lengths clear of the nearest other runner, a good distance in a five-furlong race. Maddock, van Cutsem, and Bell were delighted with him. 'He can't be the sort of horse who needs a lot of work,' van Cutsem decided, 'because he hasn't been getting any.' The Form Book ratings, which affect a horse's future starting price and give an independent estimate of his performance, described him as 'Always prominent, ran on well.'

Bernard van Cutsem thought that Mountain Call could have won the Parth Maiden Stakes if the distance had been a little greater, so he entered him next in a six-furlong race: the Kennett Maiden Stakes at Newbury, a good galloping track in Berkshire, on June 15th. None of the great races are run here, but the level of sport is high and the course and amenities are so well laid out that it is very popular with the public.

There were fifteen runners in the Kennett, including a colt called Berber, who was to become one of the finest sprinters in the country. Mountain Call's last appearance had impressed the public so much that they made him favourite. Russ Maddock rode, as usual.

Mountain Call was well placed from the start of the race, lying just in behind the leading bunch in a nice position for challenging. Maddock let the good pace set by the group ahead sweep him along for a while, but when he asked for an extra effort to move up into the narrow gap between the leaders his mount stiffened and would not face it. Unable to get Mountain Call to close up into the gap, Maddock had to change tactics and pull him out and round the outside of the field. Mountain Call responded bravely with a strong late challenge and almost caught the fast-finishing Berber at the post. The result was Mountain Call second to Berber by half a length.

Maddock thought this was a splendid performance for a green colt, and said so to van Cutsem when reporting Mountain Call's reluctance to move up between the other horses. The trainer thought that most horses by Whistler needed to wear blinkers* to make them concentrate, and decided to run Mountain Call in blinkers in the future so that he would not be able to see how close he was to the runners on each side of him.

---

* Blinkers are panels beside a horse's eyes to stop him from looking sideways or behind. They are worn by horses who are either shy of racing or who cannot be made to concentrate on it. A common practice (never done at Stanley House) is to 'gee them up' at home the first time the blinkers are put on – the horse is given a couple of belts with a whip to teach it that the blinkers mean it has got to run. Often the horse is given another belt at the racetrack in the saddling stalls when the blinkers are put on. The results can be remarkable.

Mountain Call may have had another reason to feel shy. He had been struck into from behind during the race by the sharp racing plate of another horse, and had come into the Winners' Enclosure bleeding from a cut on the off-hind fetlock.

Summer

TOWARDS the end of June, when the grass was well up in the Woodlands paddocks and the mares and foals had mostly left the stud, Indolent, She Wolf, and Bikini were brought back into training. After their idle months of play the fillies looked extremely well. Although they had not been regularly groomed their coats had a healthy gloss, and She Wolf in particular looked promising. She was a pretty filly with dark dapples on her coat and a graceful, well-proportioned body. Van Cutsem thought her easily the best classic prospect of the three.

Since the fillies had not been ridden for nearly four months, they were lunged in their saddles for a couple of days before their lads began to ride them again. Horses have good memories, and the lessons went fairly smoothly. The main difficulty lay in getting the fillies to settle down and treat work as something serious.

Indolent had a change of lad. While she had been out at grass her former lad had left Stanley House Stables and she was now taken over by George Douglas. In contrast to van Cutsem, who had a low opinion of her, Douglas had always thought her one of the pick of the two-year-olds. In discussions with other lads he had conceded that she had a plain head, but he had argued that her body was workmanlike. When one of his horses had left the yard the month before, he had asked van Cutsem if he could wait to take on Indolent when she came back. Seeing his very real enthusiasm for the filly, the trainer readily agreed.

Douglas soon became attached to Indolent, who was affectionate and loved being petted and having her ears pulled. Each day he brought her a packet of Polo mints as a treat. In turn she became so fond of him that she would lick his hands and face. He got used to the little differences that set her apart from every other horse he had worked with, and learned that she had some curious habits. After exercise, when the horses were allowed to eat a bit of grass before going back to the stables, Douglas would take off her saddle and let her roll. When she had finished, instead of getting up and shaking in the normal way, she would sit up like a dog for a moment or two, her backside planted in the grass and her forelegs stretched out in front of her. She had a passion for dandelion flowers, which she ate almost exclusively when she was supposed to be picking grass.

The fillies went out with the second lot. The older horses and the more advanced two-year-olds exercised in the first lot because van Cutsem wanted to see the important ones before he left for the races. Mountain Call always went out with the first lot. He was entered in the Gold Star Stakes at Chester on July 8th, a six-furlong sprint, since he had shown that he needed the extra distance, and he would be run in blinkers.

The Gold Star Stakes was worth £841.20 to the winner, and Mountain Call, who looked fit and keen, was made hot favourite at 5–2 on. He jumped out of the stalls into the lead full of zest, and Maddock pulled him back a little because he did not want to make the running. Two-and-a-half furlongs from home he let Mountain Call go. They came steadily away from the rest of the field and won easily by five lengths.

Mountain Call returned home to cheers from the stable, who had put their money on him.

II

The training grounds at Newmarket had dried out under the summer sun, but there was perfect going on the watered gallops. Many of van Cutsem's horses — all those who were winding up for a race — worked there at a charge of £2 a day for each horse. 'It's well worth it,' van Cutsem said. 'You can't race a horse if you can't work him first, and you can't work him if he's going to get jarred up on hard ground. A horse that is jarred up loses his action. It may take months to put him right.'

Early in July Laureate became difficult to handle. He had grown up a lot and had begun to think about whether or not he really wanted to gallop. Almost every day he would stop at some point in the exercise and refuse to go. Often he would spin round and try to go the other way. He began to object to working on certain parts of Newmarket Heath; going into these canters he would rear up, whip round and sometimes run backwards. From the moment he got on his back, Matty McCormack could always tell what sort of mood Laureate was in and whether he was likely to misbehave.

Van Cutsem took it upon himself to cure Laureate's bad behaviour. On the Stanley House gallops he walked behind the colt with a black umbrella, which he opened suddenly if Laureate whipped round or backed. 'It's a surprisingly effective way of getting a horse to go,' the trainer said. 'From Laureate's point of view, it's a big black thing behind him which flies open with a bang.'

This unorthodox treatment worked wonderfully. The umbrella certainly made Laureate go; it also set off all the other horses in the string. When Laureate objected to working on parts of the Heath, which was common land, the umbrella was again used to good effect.

Stan Warren understood Laureate's problems because he had seen them so often in other horses. 'When horses first start learning to race the sooner they are introduced to a racecourse the less trouble you'll get at home because they are less bored,' he said. 'They'll settle at home because the point of their work becomes clearer. A lot of horses are ruined by not being raced earlier. They learn bad habits, mooching about without point.'

Van Cutsem agreed. 'Colts, especially, ought to go on a racecourse,' he said. 'Laureate's a tricky character to work with. Maybe a race will take his mind off his normal routine.'

Since it seemed obvious that Laureate would benefit from a race, van Cutsem had him entered for the Plantation Maiden Stakes at Newmarket on July 13th. The colt's physical condition was excellent, and the trainer had no worries that the seven-furlong extended gallop would do him any harm. Warren elaborated on the reasons why Laureate should be raced: 'Though Lord Derby's horses are always raced to win, they are initially also raced for experience and to put their minds at rest about racing. It's like a human going to learn a new job — it takes a few times before he gets used to it. The first time he's on a racetrack the horse is seeing things he's never seen before. He's looking about him and learning. Some horses need at least three races before they begin to go about it in a workmanlike way. Others grasp what they have to do immediately. A few never learn.'

Laureate's first race was unremarkable. Ridden by Doug Smith, he finished sixth of the eleven runners. The official report afterwards described him as 'strong, compact, a bit backward, no headway final two furlongs', which meant that Laureate had looked good and probably meant that he had not really extended himself. He profited from the race as the trainer and head lad had hoped he would, settling more readily into his work and showing more enthusiasm. Matty McCormack had hoped that the race would also cure some of Laureate's more unpleasant mannerisms, but it did not. He was still a difficult ride at home, but he was beginning to see that there was some point to the work that he was doing.

Mountain Call ran again in the Home Ale Stakes at Nottingham on July 15th, carrying the top weight of 127 pounds. It was another six-furlong race and the going was firm. He started clear favourite at 9–4 on, and alarmed Maddock by swerving sideways as he came out of the starting stalls and letting the other five runners get ahead of him. Maddock gave him a good tap with his whip to get him into line and thereafter only needed to threaten with his voice. Mountain Call quickly made up his lost ground. Two furlongs from home he swept past the field to lead. He held on easily, winning by two lengths. His earnings were £1,331.10 and a great deal of goodwill from his stable.

Thus, before the summer was half over, Mountain Call had proved himself and Laureate was looking promising.

Gamecourt, meanwhile, had been coming on very slowly. He was the sort of two-year-old who is difficult to build up, who does not put on weight easily and who can quickly lose it if given too much fast work.

But he was a kind ride and an honest worker and van Cutsem

hoped he might be strong enough to get in a race or two at the back end of the season. His hopes of that soon disappeared: one morning towards the end of July, cantering on the home gallops, Gamecourt, without warning, went dead lame. His lad dismounted and led him back to the stable yard. Gamecourt limped very badly, hating to put his off-hind foot on the ground. The veterinary surgeon was sent for, though no one had any doubt about what was wrong, and Gamecourt was X-rayed and a split pastern diagnosed. This is a hairline fracture of the bone which runs from the fetlock, or ankle, of the horse down to the hoof.

Split pasterns are fairly common in racehorses – common enough for everyone at Stanley House to recognize what was wrong before a professional opinion was given – but the accident raised the individual consideration of whether treatment was worthwhile. The problems in treating fractured or broken bones are largely economic. A split pastern, while not very difficult to heal, will mean that the patient is confined to its loosebox for six months; how much will it cost to keep during this time? Will it ever be sound enough to race? If not, has it any value at stud, and will the broken bone heal well enough to keep the animal from being in pain? Gamecourt's youth and good breeding reprieved him.

A plaster-of-paris cast was wrapped around Gamecourt's pastern for support. Although the fracture was not severe, the cast had to be unusually strong because of the forces involved when the colt put his weight on this small bone. The healing process of the fracture, as with any broken bone, would be the gradual growth of new bone known as callus. Callus begins as soft tissue, rather like scar tissue, in which calcium deposits build up to make it hard. When the callus is completely formed the once-split bone is as strong as, if not stronger than, before.

Callus takes about half a year to harden, and it is essential that during this time the fractured pieces of the bone are not able to move. Gamecourt faced a monotonous six months in his box. His food was cut right down and he was given only very light mashes and hay. Any chance of his racing as a two-year-old was now quite gone.

III

Horse racing varies considerably from country to country. While British horses are trained in private stable yards and are sent off to race meetings by horsebox, American and Canadian horses are mostly trained on the racetracks where they will race. This is because America is so big: shipping horses about for a day at New York, or Florida, or California is seldom worthwhile.

American race meetings last much longer than the usual British maximum of five days; the extreme example is Hollywood Park, in California, where race meetings run for seventy-five consecutive days. Hollywood Park has stabling for about 1,400 horses, and just down the road at Santa Anita there are another 1,200 looseboxes, which are used at the same time. Most American tracks are uniform: left-handed dirt tracks on level ground, easy to maintain because they don't get cut up by flying hooves; but turf racing is becoming more popular because it is prettier to watch. Dirt tracks are still essential in America because of the length of the meetings — a turf course could not stand up to the wear of several weeks of continuous racing. There is a curious exception to dirt-track racing at Calder Park, Florida, which has a mile-long synthetic track. The surface is poured on like hot treacle, and is washed and patched when necessary. (Calder Park is not popular with jockeys because there is no give in this odd surface if they fall off.)

American tracks are, in general, alike, so the stop-watch timing of American horses makes sense. In England, where undulations in the track and variations in the going – the firmness or softness of the turf – affect the speed of the horses, the stop-watch has little significance.

American racehorses are broken in earlier and raced more often than their English counterparts. Most U.S. breeding farms have their own training tracks and starting stalls, and yearlings are often broken and ridden at a half-speed gallop before being sent up to the sales. The Keeneland Yearling Sales are in July, the Saratoga Sales in August, so American yearlings are backed in June – four months earlier than in Britain. In Florida and on the West Coast, two-year-olds are raced as early as January 1st, though the races are only three furlongs long.

The inducement in America is good prize money, while in Britain horses can earn far greater sums at stud than is possible on the track. This means that American horses race much more often than British horses, perhaps thirty times a year, and may be kept in training until they are five or six. These horses, naturally, tend to break down more easily than British horses, who run only seven or eight times a season (unless they are exceptionally tough), and retire to stud when they are three or four. The difference in the number of races has a lot to do with the tiring travelling that British horses must do, and some British trainers feel that shipping a horse to and from a meeting takes as much out of him as the actual race.

American trainers, whose horses may be working at three or more different tracks simultaneously, have an even tougher job than British trainers, and they are seldom at home, mostly living like gypsies in motels and aeroplanes. The American racing season goes on relentlessly all the year round. A trainer is likely to live in Florida from January to the end of March, then move up to New York (Belmont and Aqueduct) in the spring. In August there is the Saratoga meeting in upper New York State, and the trainer may meanwhile be running horses in Chicago; or flying one across for a big race on the West Coast; or living temporarily at Hollywood Park. Then it is back to New York in the fall, and at the end of November everyone on the East Coast – horses, lads, trainers, jockeys, punters – traipses down to Florida again.

No government in any country in the world subsidizes racing, yet most do very well out of it. In New York State, however, the Federal Government gets nothing from racing, while the state takes about 8 per cent of the betting turnover and the racetracks another 7 per cent. The rest is returned to the punter – and the New Yorker is indeed a serious punter. In 1969, for example, the betting turnover in New York State was $1,539,000,000. $164,000,000 of that went back into racing, and about the same amount to the state. By contrast, British racing suffers from the ludicrous situation in which the government makes about £60,000,000 a year, only about £4,000,000 of which goes back into the sport.

The French are much cleverer: about £45,000,000 a year goes to the government in betting tax, and roughly another £38,000,000 is ploughed back into racing. Thus French racing generates its own prize money, which is the highest in the world (entry fees for horses are very high, too). Horses that are bred in France pay 10 per cent of their winnings to the breeder, which encourages good racehorse breeders to move to France. On the racecourses, entrance money for spectators is minimal, and much time and thought is spent on such pleasant extras as attractive flowerbeds. So, having enticed its audience with a small entry fee and a day out in pretty surroundings, the French Government makes its money in betting tax from the Tote monopoly (no bookmakers are allowed in France).

French racehorses, like English horses, are trained in private yards and not at the racetracks – or not for long. Racing stables are mostly at Chantilly and Maisons-Laffitte, near Paris, but a winter season at Cagnes-sur-Mer, near Nice, takes some of the horses south for several weeks. Paris empties in the hottest part of the summer, and racing moves to Deauville, on the north coast, for a six-week season. Facilities for board and lodging at Deauville are extensive, and horses often stay there for the full six weeks, working on grass tracks or on the sand.

The fat French purses often lure the best of the British horses across the Channel. Although there is more prestige attached to winning a £500 race in England, where the emphasis is on winners and placed horses do not count for much, a third or fourth place at Longchamp is often more rewarding financially for the owner. Mountain Call's impressive performance in the Home Ale Stakes and the Gold Star Stakes led his trainer to feel that he had a good chance of picking up £16,639 in the Prix Mornay at Deauville on August 20th.

Mountain Call was flown over more than a week before the Mornay to give him a chance to get acclimatized to France. To get experience of the Deauville racetrack he was entered for the Criterion du Bernay on August 12th. His own food and water were flown over with him because any change in diet could affect his racing performance. Deauville is a seaside course and Russ Maddock was glad to be able to take his wife and children with him for the ten-day stay. While the young Maddocks splashed about in the sea, their father and Mountain Call ambled down to the post for the Criterion du Bernay and romped home. They won the six-furlong race by one-and-a-half lengths, picking up a further £2,277.50 in prize money. It was the first time Maddock had won in France, and Mountain Call had given him a thrilling ride. 'I can't think of any greater pleasure than riding a good horse in a race,' he said afterwards. He was a happy man.

Arthur Bell had also travelled over with Mountain Call. During the week between the two races he took him out for his normal work, trying to make him feel as much at home as possible. Van Cutsem had given him written instructions on precisely what to do to have the colt in fine shape for the Mornay. Mountain Call seemed unmoved by the change of location, and on the day of the big race looked marvellously well. He sauntered down to the post in his usual lazy way and went into the stalls at the first time of asking. But when Maddock set about keying him up for the race, Mountain Call did not respond. He did not wake up in the stalls, nor did he wake up during the race. He finished out of the first six and seemed still asleep when Maddock, puzzled and disappointed, rode him back to the unsaddling enclosure.

There was soon a discussion about Mountain Call's poor performance. Bernard van Cutsem, who had flown over for the race, had been talking to some trainers from Chantilly who explained that in their experience horses left at Deauville tended to become lazy because of the sea air, much as a week at the seaside will affect human beings on holiday. He blamed himself for not having had Mountain Call sent home to England between the races.

Russ Maddock had been the most surprised. He had thought nothing of Mountain Call's pre-race laziness because it was perfectly in character, and had been quite sure that he would wake up as usual when expected to work.

On August 21st Mountain Call was flown back to Cambridge airport and taken in the horsebox to Stanley House Stables. It was a sunny day, cold for August, when Mountain Call came home to a disappointed stable. He was given a warm mash, and next day he went out for light work.

IV

The fillies had been back in training for more than two months, and Indolent and She Wolf were now forward enough to make van Cutsem think about racing them. Indolent was plain and sturdy, but an honest worker. She Wolf had all the looks but she was nervous and temperamental, though she had calmer, stubborn moods when in season. She would bite and kick strangers who did not know how to handle her. Bikini never bit anyone, nor did she ever throw her rider at exercise; on the contrary, she was very quiet, lazy, and kind. She was, however, still backward and overgrown.

She Wolf was a sharp worker. Maureen Foley thought her a nice ride, though as she was worked up into training she became so keen that it was difficult to hold her on the gallops. After each gallop She Wolf blew excessively. The noise at first worried Maureen, but since the laboured breathing did not seem to affect the filly's performance she learned to ignore it.

Indolent was the first to have a race, in the Tadcaster Maiden Stakes at York on September 7th. It was a six-furlong race in soft going, and Indolent, ridden by Doug Smith, finished tenth of the nineteen runners. The Form Book commented 'good sort, strong', but van Cutsem was not impressed with her.

The St Leger meeting, the biggest English racing event of the month, was held at Doncaster in the second week of September. Mountain Call, She Wolf, and Laureate were all entered. Mountain Call was to run on the thirteenth, the day of the big race, in the Norfolk Stakes, She Wolf on the fourteenth in the Devonshire Maiden Stakes, and Laureate on the fifteenth in the Feversham Maiden Stakes. Mountain Call's race was only a five-furlong one, which was not thought to be far enough for him, but the prize money of £3,000 was enticing. He finished second to the good two-year-old D'Urberville, who had been successful over five furlongs in the past. Mountain Call had run a good race, but had been unable to get on terms with D'Urberville in such a short distance.

She Wolf's first appearance on a track was in a good-class race, the Devonshire Maiden Stakes, run over six furlongs and worth £1,000. A maiden race is one in which none of the runners has ever won a race; however, all but one of the eight others in the field had raced before, and She Wolf was opposed by some high-class fillies. She seemed nervous in the paddock, but her bay coat shone in the sun and she looked so well that she was made joint third favourite at 100-9. She snorted as she cantered down to the start, mildly upset by the strange surroundings. The noisy Doncaster crowd frightened her, and Doug Smith, who was riding, had to use a lot of tact to get her into the stalls. He had just begun to gather her under him ready to leap out for the start when the gates in front flew open prematurely. Someone had accidentally touched the starting button. Most of the fillies jumped out from habit and had to be turned back and reloaded. It was most unfortunate: these maiden fillies, who were not experienced racehorses, were only just learning to jump out of the stalls and were certainly not mature enough to understand why they should be stopped instead of encouraged to go on, or why they should have to go back into the stalls again. Some of them, reasonably, objected to this and the horse handlers had a good deal of pushing and shoving to do to get the nine runners reloaded.

In the event, the race started only three minutes late. She Wolf struck out of the stalls fast and ran so strongly that she took up the lead after two furlongs and kept it until headed by Pardina, the favourite, a hundred and fifty yards from the winning post. She held on well to keep second place, five lengths clear of the rest of the field. As usual after a gallop, she pulled up making a nasty noise in the wind, but she did not seem in any way distressed. The Form Book's opinion, 'promising, well grown, good sort', was an understatement of what Stanley House thought of her.

Laureate, running at Doncaster the following day, also pleased his stable. In the seven-furlong Feversham Maiden Stakes he finished fifth of sixteen runners, beaten just over three lengths by some very promising two-year-olds. Vaguely Noble, who was second, later won the Prix de l'Arc de Triomphe, the richest race in Europe; Ribero, fourth, went on to win the Irish Sweeps Derby and the St Leger. Laureate was close up with this good company until approaching the final furlong, when he weakened.

Soon after this van Cutsem was asked which of his two-year-olds were the most likely classic prospects. He replied unhesitatingly, 'Laureate and She Wolf.' It was too early for him to feel sure of anything, and so far all of the youngsters – even Gamecourt, whose disability should have righted itself in time for the next racing season – looked promising. Stan Warren thought them as nice a crop of two-year-olds as the stable had ever had.

Bikini and Indolent were the least exciting. There was even a possibility that Lord Derby might want to sell them at the end of the year.

Autumn

COUGHING broke out at Stanley House; not a serious epidemic, but enough to prevent a lot of the horses from cantering, since cantering with a cough can cause permanent damage to a horse's wind. Nearly all of the two-year-olds coughed for the last two weeks of September. Laureate only coughed once or twice, but She Wolf caught it fairly badly, and Indolent and Bikini were mildly affected.

Van Cutsem decided to turn the fillies away again. The coughs would have to clear up before they could race, and the racing season had only another six weeks to run. The weather was warm and mild, and he knew that the fillies would enjoy a couple of months of grass and play. Indolent and She Wolf had already had a taste of racing, which was all that was expected of them as two-year-olds. Bikini would have to finish her two-year-old season unraced.

The trainer would have preferred to give a holiday to the colts too, but they were all fairly conscious of themselves as stallions and he could not trust them not to fight in the paddocks.

Mountain Call, unaffected by the cough, was in magnificent condition. 'He's a charming horse to deal with,' van Cutsem said. 'He's tough, and he's consistent. He can't be the sort that needs much work at home – he's still so idle on the Heath that he packs it in after about two-and-a-half furlongs.' On the racetrack he was a different horse. He romped away with the Junior Trust Stakes, worth £2,000, at Ascot on September 29th. He carried five pounds more than anything else in the field and won by two-and-a-half lengths, having made all the running. On October 21st, the top weight by 9 pounds, he won the Suffolk Nursery Handicap at Newmarket. A nursery handicap is a race in which all of the entrants have run two or three times, or at least often enough for the handicapper to have some idea of their form.

The handicapper's job is to allot weights so that, all other factors being equal, the runners all pass the finishing post together. The handicapper in the Suffolk had guessed well: Pussy Pelmet, second to Mountain Call by half a length, was carrying 36 pounds less. A half-length difference between two horses is reckoned at $1\frac{1}{2}$ pounds. A pound of weight is also reckoned in time at $\frac{1}{15}$ of a second. So the Suffolk handicapper had misjudged the two winners by only $\frac{1}{10}$ of a second.

Handicaps are based on past performances, but in cases where horses have not previously been raced there is also a Scale of Weight for Age, which gives the weights at which an average two-year-old may reasonably meet a three-, four-, or five-year-old on equal terms, the older horse having the advantage of strength. This scale was to affect Mountain Call in his next race. At the start of the racing season horses are handicapped with lighter weights than at the end because they are weaker; thus a two-year-old and a three-year-old in a five-furlong race in April will carry 84 pounds and 116 pounds respectively, whereas in November they will carry 110 pounds and 125 pounds. Weight allowances between horses of different ages are greater at the start of the season than at the end, and the amount of weight given by the older horse increases with the distance of the race. In a five-furlong race in November a two-year-old receives 15 pounds from a three-year-old, whereas if the race is over two miles the difference in weights is 31 pounds. All this is theoretical because it assumes that, ages apart, the horses are exactly equal, but the weight that a young horse is required to carry is usually a fair indication of its form. The allowance for a length between two horses at the finish is three pounds. For a neck or head it is one pound. Trainers make, or lose, their money when they feel that a handicapper has treated one of their horses over-generously.

Mountain Call had been entered for the Vernons' November Sprint Cup at Haydock Park, Lancashire, on November 4th, the last day of the flat season. It was a six-furlong race with a first prize of £4,281, the most valuable weight-for-age race of the season. The favourite was a three-year-old colt called Be Friendly, of whom Jim Snow, Racing Correspondent of *The Times*, had written: 'Be Friendly is something more than the champion sprinter. He can claim to be as tough, resolute, and consistent a horse as there is in training.' Be Friendly was weighted to give Mountain Call 18 pounds – exactly the difference between them on the weight-for-age scale. Mountain Call, at the end of his first season, had become theoretically the equal of the champion sprinter.

The going at Haydock had been softened by heavy rain and it was wet on the day of the race. Mountain Call struck out of the stalls fast and after 2½ furlongs took up the lead. Soon Be Friendly came past and got his head in front. Mountain Call fought back, Maddock riding for his life. Neither was willing to give in. The race became a match between the two colts, who drew clear of the rest of the field. They passed the post together, five lengths clear. The photograph gave it to Be Friendly by a neck.

Maddock was ecstatic. 'A marvellous run,' he said. 'A truly spectacular effort for a two-year-old.' Van Cutsem was full of admiration, and Arthur Bell was quite light-headed. Mountain Call had done very well by Bell. Apart from the bets which love and faith had made him place on the colt, he had money that Mr Kornberg, Mountain Call's owner, had given him for looking after the colt so well. (Van Cutsem was very good at getting presents for his lads from the owners. For a winner of a race worth under £1,000 he would usually contrive to have the lad given £35. For a race worth more than £1,000 it would be £55. For an exceptionally good race it was sometimes more.)

At the end of the flat season the Jockey Club's official handicapper makes an assessment of the best two-year-olds of the season, on the supposition that *if* all of the most promising horses were to race together the following spring, and *if* they maintained their two-year-old form, he would give them weights that would make them all finish together. The handicapper's opinion is published in the Free Handicap, which appears in December, and is of general interest because its weights sum up the two-year-old performance of the horses. Mountain Call was rated at 120 pounds, joint twelfth most promising two-year-old in England.

Most of the Free Handicap horses placed above Mountain Call were classic horses. Petingo headed the list with 133 pounds. The French Free Handicap had Cabhurst at the top, with 132 pounds, and the Irish had a clear lead in their handicap (doubtless because they allowed a heavier top weight) with a colt called Sir Ivor, who had not yet been seen in England. Sir Ivor was rated at 140 pounds, and was winter favourite for the Derby.

Another two-year-old assessment that concerned Mountain Call was the flat speed figures published by the Form Book at the end of the season. These were based on optimum times, and showed the speed figures at 126 pounds after allowances had been made for the going. Only the best horses were included; 95 was the lowest figure given, 126 the highest. Mountain Call rated 118 for his run in the Vernons' November Sprint. Only seven other two-year-olds had faster times. She Wolf just scraped in at 95, but none of Lord Derby's other horses qualified.

II

At the end of the flat season Doug Smith retired. In a long and brilliant career as a jockey he had been champion five times, and now planned to become a trainer. He had taken out a licence and had had his own stables built in Newmarket. Lord Derby had promised to send him a few horses, and so had other owners for whom he had ridden. The popular Smith would be greatly missed at Stanley House.

Willie Carson, understudy to Smith in the summer, was now appointed first jockey to Lord Derby. At twenty-five, he was a promising young jockey who had developed late. In 1957, when he was fifteen, Carson had been apprenticed to Gerald Armstrong, who trained in Yorkshire; when Armstrong retired in 1962, Carson's indentures were transferred to his brother, Fred Armstrong, at Newmarket. Both Armstrongs had given him rides in apprentice races, and he rode his first winner in 1961, when he was nineteen. It was his only win of the season. The following season he rode five winners.

Apprenticeships are usually finished by the time a man is

twenty-one, but since Carson had by then ridden only six winners he continued his apprenticeship for a further two years. He was pretty sure that no trainer except Armstrong would give him rides with only six wins to his credit. Armstrong's confidence in Carson turned out to be justified. He rode sixteen winners in 1963, thirty-five the next year, and thirty-seven in 1965. In July 1966 he was approached by Lord Derby in the sort of roundabout way that would give him time to think. Derby spoke to Armstrong, and Armstrong spoke to Carson in the tack room. 'Don't decide now,' Armstrong said. 'Think it over for a couple of weeks.' Carson said later that he had thought it over for a couple of seconds. First jockey to Lord Derby meant he would be riding top-class horses trained by a top-class trainer; he and his wife, Carol, would be given a nice house on the Stanley House estate; he would be paid a retainer to ride Lord Derby's horses and would be allowed to ride for other owners if he was free. This was his chance to get to the top of his profession.

In 1967 Carson was given eight of Lord Derby's horses to ride. None of them was expected to do well, but it gave him a chance to work into replacing Smith. He rode out for van Cutsem three times a week, always on Derby's horses, and spent most of the time watching the other horses so that he could get to know what they could do. He watched them in races as well, at the track and on television. On the days when he was not riding for van Cutsem he continued to ride for Armstrong. By the end of the season he felt he had an acceptable knowledge of his new job.

On November 8th, four days after the end of the flat, Carson had a car accident. He drove into a wagon which was doing a U-turn on the Great North Road in a fog. He fractured the femur in his right leg and smashed his right ankle, broke his jaw and knocked out his front teeth, and broke his index finger. He needed thirty-seven stitches in his face. He had been planning to take Carol away for a holiday. Instead, he spent the winter in hospital.

III

The first forfeit stage for the 1968 classics came round on November 21st. Bernard van Cutsem took Bikini out of the One Thousand Guineas and the St Leger. He left all the others in. Bikini's liability for these two races had come to £40.

IV

The fillies had come back into training in mid-November, since it was getting too cold to leave them standing out in the paddocks. Indolent and Bikini had been reprieved and were to stay on at Stanley House. This time it was Bikini who was without a lad. Her former lad had given her up because he did not think she had any ability. A very young apprentice named Raymond Coppola asked if he could look after her and was given permission to do so.

Ray Coppola was only just sixteen. He had been riding for less than a year and knew very little about racehorses. Coppola lived in the Stanley House hostel with the other apprentices, working for board and lodging and 87½p a week. In the first ten months of his apprenticeship he had had no free time, but then he had been given ten days off to go and visit his parents. He loved racing, he loved Bikini, and he wanted to learn.

Bikini was ideal. 'She taught me to understand racehorses,' Coppola said. 'Her temperament was so kind that you could do anything with her. I used to slip back to her box when work was finished and talk to her. She would let me sit on her head or her hindquarters when she was lying down, and I could ride her around the box without any tack on. I certainly wasn't supposed to do this, but I couldn't resist it. When we led in from exercise she would follow behind me like a dog.'

Bikini was as kind to ride as she was in the stable. She used sometimes to buck when exercising, but she did it so comfortably that nobody ever fell off her. 'It was like riding a rocking horse,' Coppola said.

In the first weeks of Coppola's work with Bikini he found that the woollen sweaters he wore in the stables were wearing badly. Holes kept appearing in the backs, though there were no other signs of wear. After a while he solved the mystery; Bikini liked wool. She ate through three of his sweaters from the back while he was cleaning out her manger, and did it so gently that he never realized what was happening.

Laureate had also been abandoned, because McCormack had transferred to another racing stable. No one wanted to do him; he was churlish and proud, and would chase people out of his box. In the end, Warren assigned him to a lad named Tony Leaman who had ridden him once or twice and had seemed to get on well with him.

The big difference from this point on was that Leaman was not affected by Laureate's beastly behaviour; in fact, he did not seem to notice it. When asked about his colt's character, he said mildly that Laureate was 'a bit kinky'. Laureate tried his old trick of whipping round at exercise; Leaman found that if he let him do so on a slack rein the colt would come to hand easily. He liked Laureate, and on most evenings would bring him a handful of grass. By the end of the year Laureate was very quiet in the box. Even the farrier said so.

1968

Winter

SNOW fell at Newmarket. The horses exercised in the covered school and everyone was bored again. In the middle of January the veterinary surgeon announced that Gamecourt's pastern had healed enough for exercise, and the colt was allowed to go outside for the first time in six months. His body and neck were gaunt and his liver-chestnut coat was shaggy and dull. For the last half year he had been on a very light diet, and had not needed to have his coat clipped to keep him from sweating at exercise. He had hardly been groomed at all during his confinement because grooming would have removed the oils needed to maintain a healthy coat, and he would not have been able to replace them by exercising himself. He was delighted with the open air.

Jack Banks, who had ridden work on him as a two-year-old and had liked the way he moved, was glad to see him out again. He asked Bernard van Cutsem if he could do him and was given permission. In his first days of freedom Gamecourt was exercised gently, and he was led out at a walk, at first unsaddled and then with Banks on him and a man to lead him. He wanted to run and buck, but could not be allowed to do so on his newly-healed leg. After three weeks he was strong enough to trot with the string. Like Bikini, he was such a kind ride that the apprentices often used to ride him.

By the third week of February the bigger colts had started galloping again. Occasional falls of snow and some sharp frosts sometimes held them up, but the weather did not seriously interrupt their work. Laureate had been entered for the Union Jack Stakes at Liverpool at the end of March, and Mountain Call was down for the Ascot Two Thousand Guineas Trial Stakes on April 15th.

Lord Derby came to spend a few days at Stanley House. In the cold early mornings, he went out with his trainer, eager to see how his horses were getting on. He took a great interest in all of them, always knowing what they had done and what their capabilities were. His ambition, as ever, was to win the Derby with a horse he had bred himself, and this year his hopes lay mainly with Laureate, since Gamecourt was still untried.

Stable jockeys began to appear on the Heath again, some of them actually migrants from warmer countries where flat racing was held in winter. Maddock came back, riding the jockeyless Derby horses while Carson sat on at home with his leg strapped up. Since Carson had no chance of being strong enough to ride by the beginning of the season, Maddock was to deputize for him.

Before first light each morning Warren was out checking that the horses had eaten up. Horses that have started galloping tend to go off their feed until after their first race, and Warren expected to find a few mangers that were not quite clean. But work made no difference to Mountain Call's boundless appetite, and Warren had no need to check Bikini either, except to put back the rugs that she so often managed to get off over her head during the night. She Wolf ate a little less than the others and after a hard gallop would leave most of her food, which worried Warren. She still made a noise after working, but she never seemed distressed.

Indolent did well, though she could be a little finicky and

needed enticing if for any reason she had been fed more than usual. She gave herself additional exercise by parading around her box during the day. In the evenings, tied up waiting for van Cutsem's inspection, she would scrape up her bedding with a forefoot. This made Warren think she worried, but George Douglas thought she was only restless.

The crocuses came out and the first daffodils began to bloom. Early spring appealed to Laureate. One morning on the Severalls he dislodged Leaman and ran all over the flower beds.

II

All over England, flat courses were being prepared for the new season. The turf was fertilized, harrowed, and rolled with a spike roller to aerate the roots. On courses where early meetings were planned, the grass was cut to a height of three to four inches. It had last been cut before the autumn frosts, which stop the grass from growing.

Lawns were mown, flowerbeds planted out. Painters and carpenters neatened up the grandstands, paddock railings, and the railings on the course. Stabling for visiting racehorses was thoroughly cleaned and disinfected. Hostels for the stable lads were aired, and beds made up. Caterers were alerted for forthcoming meetings.

Each racecourse makes its own security arrangements. Horses are usually locked into their boxes, and the key is given to the travelling head lad who is in charge of each runner. Guards are engaged to patrol the stable blocks at night. Floodlights are often used to keep away potential dopers.

The turf—the bread and butter of any racecourse—must

be kept in perfect condition. In dry weather, anything up to 200,000 gallons of water a day is used on a racecourse. Between each race, a squad of twenty or thirty people go out on the course treading back the cut-up turf. When the day's racing is over, treading on the course continues until the racecourse manager is satisfied. Then the whole course is ring-rolled to press the turf down. Holes are filled with a mixture of soil, peat, sand, and grass seed (if turves were laid instead they could be kicked out during a race, and might cause an accident).

On the morning of a race, the day starts early. Racecards, printed by Weatherby's, arrive at six thirty. The starting stalls, which belong to the Jockey Club, are towed in by Land-Rover. Caterers set up the bars and lunchrooms; the camera patrol, public address system, and (sometimes) television people all move in. Jockeys' valets bring their clients' equipment. The racecourse manager is everywhere, making sure that nothing has been forgotten. All too soon, the public starts to trickle in.

When the crowds have gone home, the clearing up begins. The litter of racecards and betting slips is tidied up. Bars are cleared and the caterers disappear, leaving behind a bevy of women washing up and cleaning. Laundry has to be sent off. A hundred or more stables need to be cleaned out and disinfected. The stable lads' hostel is done from top to bottom.

On most courses, the complete clearing-up operation after a race meeting takes about five days.

Spring

LAUREATE'S first race as a three-year-old, the Union Jack Stakes, was run at Liverpool on March 28th, on the flat-race course which shares the amenities of the famous Aintree jumping course. It was a perfect warm spring day and the crowd was the biggest that the meeting had seen for many years. They had sold out of racecards before the first race.

It was a mixed meeting, with three flat races and several over the sticks. The Union Jack, a race for three-year-olds over one mile, was not a valuable race, but it was interesting because it was the first race of the season to display the form of several classic entrants. Willie Carson sat at home, watching it on television. His face had healed but his leg was still in a calliper.

He watched Leaman leading Laureate, who was third favourite at 9–2, round the Paddock on a chiffney, a very severe bit normally used for stallions. 'This is the dark horse of the race,' the television reporter said. Laureate looked cool and calm. He was wearing an Australian cheeker, the sign of a puller. This is a strip of rubber fastened to the headband of the bridle and running down the front of the face, divided on the nose and attached to the bit on either side so that pressure on the reins tightens the rubber across the horse's nose.

Carson caught a glimpse of Laureate as the horses cantered down to the start. He appeared to be taking a strong hold, and

Carson guessed that Maddock must be glad of the Australian cheeker: there is nothing more embarrassing than a horse bolting before he is supposed to. The race was to be started with an old-fashioned starting gate. Laureate walked calmly around until the Starter ordered the jockeys to line up. They all came into line, but two of the runners turned around. On the second attempt they got away.

Laureate was left a bit at the start and began behind the rest of the field. He came up with them on the first bend, but was on the inside and could not find a way through. Maddock pulled him clear, and they began to pass the other runners on the outside. Entering the straight they were lying sixth. At the three-furlong marker they had moved up to fourth. Two furlongs from home Laureate drew level with the leaders and raced away to win by four lengths. He had been going very strongly all the way, and was still increasing his lead when he passed the post. Stansfield, favourite on his good two-year-old form, was second.

When he had changed his clothes, Maddock was interviewed on television. He was obviously pleased, but his words were diplomatic: 'He behaved just as we thought he would from his home work. Whether or not he turns out to be a good horse remains to be seen.'

Carson, watching at home, did not have to worry about raising the public's hopes unduly. His own hopes were very high indeed and the thought of missing more rides on such a horse depressed him. He telephoned his doctor and asked if he could start riding again, but the doctor told him that it was quite out of the question. When van Cutsem came home that night, Carson got on the telephone again. The trainer tried to dissuade him from going back to work so soon, but Carson persisted. The following day he was out on Old Dick, van Cutsem's hack.

The racing journalists had also been watching Laureate. Hotspur of the *Daily Telegraph* had this to say about him:

> The most impressive Flat race performance here this afternoon was put up by Lord Derby's classic hope Laureate. Cruising to the front with a furlong of the Union Jack Stakes left, he beat the consistent Stansfield by an easy four lengths.
>
> Laureate has now shortened in William Hill's Derby prices from 100–1 to 33–1 but it must be remembered that he received twelve pounds from Stansfield today. Remand, England's leading Derby candidate, finished more than eight lengths in front of Stansfield when they met at Ascot last autumn.
>
> Laureate, therefore, needs to continue improving fast.

The Times, also with an eye on classic form, said this: 'What we came to regard as our best two-year-old form last season was in no way devalued yesterday. ... In time we may realize that it was no disgrace to be beaten four lengths by Laureate.

'He is obviously a nice horse in the making – just how good is anyone's guess.'

II

Each afternoon Willie Carson rode about on Old Dick, pulling himself out of the feebleness caused by a winter of immobility. He steamed off some of his fat in a sauna bath he had had built in his garden, and after a few days felt strong enough to go out with the string for exercise and got back to riding racehorses. He was frightened that his leg would break again and was careful how he used it. He noticed for the first time that when a mount of his ducked a shoulder he kept his balance by putting weight on his legs.

As always, he was watching all of Derby's horses. Now, for the first time, he was able to ride the new three-year-olds. The light-framed Gamecourt had come on tremendously well. He had got over his split pastern much earlier than expected and was looking almost a hundred per cent well. He was a splendid worker and a good lead horse, cantering along in front of the string at just the required pace. Bikini was still babyish in character but strong to look at. Her only physical fault was that she was very straight in the pasterns and stood over at the joints, so that her legs looked too stiff and straight to give her an easy, flexible galloping action.

Carson found that She Wolf took a strong hold at a canter. She was taking a long time to cast her winter coat and looked shaggier than the others. Indolent he liked, mainly because of her temperament. 'She's a sweet, pleasant filly,' he said, 'a real *female* type.' Laureate, Carson discovered, worked well enough once he got going, but tended to be initially stubborn. He would whip round, but would telegraph his rider first. 'You could see him thinking and know when he was going to do it,' Carson said.

Stan Warren thought them the best lot the stable had had for several years. Carson could not really tell; he fancied all of Lord Derby's horses because they were the first lot he had had to himself.

One morning, when the string was working on the race-course side of the town, it began to rain. Carson was looking forward to a bit of sharp work on Laureate and hoping the ground would not get greasy. A few bystanders had come out to watch the horses. One of them opened a big black umbrella. Laureate, remembering the summer before, took off across the Heath.

Most horses are a little lazy at home, though some will go better there than on a racecourse because they are more relaxed. Mountain Call was still exceptionally lazy, but was having to do a lot of work to get fit for the Two Thousand Guineas Trial on April 5th in which he was to meet the much-vaunted Sir Ivor, the Irish hope who was now spring favourite for the Derby. The race was to be held at Ascot, over seven furlongs. It seemed strange that a sprinter and a classic horse should meet, but Mountain Call had won over six furlongs as a two-year-old and could be expected to go further at three; Sir Ivor was bred to be a miler, and the only doubts in the minds of his Derby fanciers were that he might not manage the Derby mile and a half.

The fifth was a typical April day, windy with showers. Sir Ivor won the trial by half a length from a colt called Dalry, with Mountain Call six lengths away third. The result does not show how good a race Mountain Call ran. He had been the equal of Sir Ivor for the first five-and-a-half furlongs, and had only begun to lose ground when asked to go beyond his usual distance. If nothing else, the race established Mountain Call's best distance. He had also run, for a change, without his blinkers.

He ran next in a six-furlong race at Nottingham ten days later. It was the Ladbroke Nottingham Stakes, a mixed-age-group handicap worth £3,299 to the winner, and Mountain Call had his blinkers on again. He carried top weight of the three-year-olds, and on weight for age conceded eight pounds

to the nearest other runner. He ran an excellent race and was
well placed throughout, but could not catch the winner,
Relian, who had gone out in front early on and had held on
to his position. Relian, a four-year-old, had carried 115
pounds and Mountain Call 123 pounds, a difference of 23
pounds on the weight-for-age scale. The third horse, Morgan's
Pride, who ran Mountain Call to a short head, was a four-
year-old carrying 103 pounds. Maddock said later that
Mountain Call should not have been beaten by Relian, who
had charged the starting gate and got a six-length start,
eventually winning by two lengths. Maddock said that if it
had been a stalls start Mountain Call would have had an
advantage because he could get away from a standing start
faster than most, whereas from a moving start he was merely
average.

III

April 16th was another forfeit day for the Guineas. Van
Cutsem took Laureate out of the Two Thousand Guineas
and Indolent out of the One Thousand Guineas because he
did not think they would be ready in time. Each horse was
liable for a forfeit of £50.

IV

Carson had his first race of the season on Bikini at Newmarket, on April 16th. It was a seven-furlong race for maiden
three-year-old fillies, with a big field, and Bikini got tailed off
behind it early on. She was not interested in racing, and Carson thought her a slow, overgrown baby. The Form Book

called her 'backward', which was quite polite in the circum-
stances.

Gamecourt ran for the first time the following day, also at
Newmarket, and turned out to be almost as useless as Bikini.
It was a one-mile race for three-year-olds who had never run,
and Gamecourt looked so impressive in the Paddock that he
started second favourite of the fifteen runners. He had been
working so well at home that his stable had their money on
him.

Unfortunately, the novelty of going racing fascinated him.
He looked about him a lot in the Paddock, interested by the
crowds, the strange horses, the different atmosphere. On the
way down to the start it was just the same. Maddock, riding
because Carson's leg was giving him trouble, reported that
Gamecourt seemed to be intrigued by the strange scene. When
the jockey got to work on him as they came under Starter's
Orders he found that, far from gathering himself up for the
jump off, Gamecourt was peering up at the starting gate.

They got away fairly slowly. Maddock had orders to keep
Gamecourt behind early in the race, which was not difficult
because Gamecourt was far too interested by what was going
on to realize that he was supposed to be racing. He finished
tenth, having run very green.

At this same three-day Newmarket meeting, She Wolf
had her first race of the season on the last day, April 18th.
It was a good-class seven-furlong race for three-year-old
fillies, with a first prize of £1,182. The lads at Stanley House
thought she would probably win and had bet on her. Carson,
feeling stronger after his day's rest, fancied her too, but
could not bet because jockeys are forbidden to do so under a
ruling of the Jockey Club. The hot favourite was a filly called

Abbie West who had done very well the season before. There were only four runners. She Wolf started second favourite. She carried joint bottom weight of 118 pounds, being allowed five pounds as a maiden. Sing Again, the third favourite, had to carry 127 pounds because she had already won a race worth more than £1,000.

The four-strong field came out of the starting stalls very slowly. No one much wanted to make the running, but Carson thought he might as well take advantage of the pace as She Wolf seemed to be moving happily along in front. She had got smartly away, and led the field at least three lengths clear for most of the race. At the Bushes, two furlongs from home, Abbie West closed up to her. She Wolf ran on well, and Abbie West only managed to get on terms with her in the final furlong. The race went to Abbie West by a length, which was a great credit to She Wolf, who was a much more inexperienced racehorse.

She Wolf pulled up roaring like a bull. She seemed distressed this time, and Maureen Foley was extremely worried. Van Cutsem thought she had better be examined, and the veterinary surgeon was sent for as soon as she got home. He could find nothing wrong with her, and could only think that perhaps some curious malformation of the windpipe was causing the noise. In subsequent exercises Maureen could not feel anything wrong.

Later in the month She Wolf damaged a joint. No one could find out how she had done it, but she was definitely lame. Since the four-day declaration stage for the One Thousand Guineas came up on April 28th, She Wolf could not be declared to run, and incurred a forfeit of £80. Hopes of winning the Oaks with her on May 29th receded.

V

The Thirsk Classic Trial on April 20th was restricted to
three-year-old entire colts and fillies who were entered in
classic races. Thirsk is a pretty little track a long way out in
the country, sheltered by the hills of the North Riding of
Yorkshire. The day was perfect, with brilliant sun and a light
wind. Spring had come on early and the racetrack was a bright
green. Laureate had travelled up from Newmarket to uphold
his new reputation, and Lord Derby had come to see him do it.

The prize money was £2,500. The public, overlooking the
other runners, appeared to regard the race as a match between
Laureate and a colt called Chebs Lad, who had won five of his
nine two-year-old races, and on his first appearance as a
three-year-old the week before had had a clear victory.
Indeed, so strong was the reputation of these two colts that
they had frightened away most of the other entrants and were
opposed by only three runners. The somewhat extraordinary
betting went like this: evens Chebs Lad and Laureate, 25–1
Pettyless, 66–1 Strathallander, 100–1 Catalyst.

Most of the racing journalists were slightly in favour of
Chebs Lad, but the pieces they wrote were careful. Under the
heading LAUREATE WILL TEST CHEBS LAD TO THE FULL,
the *Sporting Life* wrote: '[Chebs Lad] will be well suited by
this course, but it should also present no real problem to the
beautifully actioned Laureate. ... He will do himself great
credit if he can give Chebs Lad a hard race over this sharp
course, and I am quite prepared to see him do so.'

Maddock was to ride, partly because van Cutsem was still
not convinced that Carson was fit and partly because it seemed

unfair to take Maddock off in favour of a man who had never raced the colt before when Maddock had done so well with Laureate at Liverpool.

Chebs Lad, Strathallander and Catalyst were very cool in the Paddock. Chebs Lad was a rakish-looking sort, built rather like a greyhound. Pettyless, who wore blinkers, sweated up. Laureate, much the handsomest of the runners, messed about, pulling at his bridle – he had the chiffney on again – and dancing sideways on the grass at the edge of the gravel ring. The race was due to start at three fifteen. At five minutes past three the jockeys entered. Maddock, in the famous black jacket and white cap, joined Derby and van Cutsem in the middle of the ring. 'Jockeys get mounted, please,' came over the loudspeakers. Michael Ryan checked the girths and Maddock was up. As before, Laureate wore an Australian cheeker.

Tony Leaman led them out onto the track and took off the lead-rein. As soon as he let go, Laureate whipped round and shot Maddock off. Leaman put Maddock up again and sent them off for a trot past the stands before they went down to the gate. Laureate did not at all want to go and show himself off. He dug his toes in and tried to whip round again, but Maddock got the better of him and forced him out in front of the crowd. Cantering down to the start, it was obvious that Laureate was taking the strongest hold of the field. Maddock rode holding him very short and had to sit against him, using his weight on the reins to keep the colt back to a canter.

It was a stalls start, and Laureate broke fast, ahead of the others. Maddock, who wanted Laureate to conserve his strength for the closing stages, took a pull at him. Laureate went out of stride and settled in at the back of the field, just

ahead of Chebs Lad. The pace was fast. Catalyst made the
running from Strathallander and Pettyless, but just after
halfway Catalyst and Pettyless tired and dropped out, leaving
Strathallander in the lead. Chebs Lad, who had been going
comfortably all the way, began to move up with three furlongs
to go. Three hundred yards from the post he took up the lead
and drew clear. Maddock, who had followed Chebs Lad when
he had moved up and had improved his position a little but
not enough, had now got his whip out. Laureate did not
accelerate. He did not like being hit, and he not only allowed
Chebs Lad to go on and win by five lengths, but also let the
66–1 outsider Strathallander beat him one-and-a-half lengths
for second place.

Chebs Lad, a favourite with northern racegoers, returned
to a tremendous ovation. No one could explain why Laureate
had been beaten so disastrously. Had he objected to being
told what to do during the race? Perhaps he was just too
slow and his Liverpool performance had been merely a piece
of luck. Michael Ryan said afterwards that he had thought
Laureate fairly beaten. 'He just couldn't go fast enough.'

VI

April 23rd was the second forfeit stage for the Derby, the
Oaks, and the St Leger. Gamecourt was struck out for the
Derby, incurring a forfeit of £80; Bikini was withdrawn from
the Oaks for £50; Indolent and Gamecourt were struck from
the St Leger at £60 each.

Lord Derby's remaining classic entries were Laureate in
the Derby, Indolent and She Wolf in the Oaks, and Laureate
and She Wolf in the St Leger.

VII

Bikini ran again on April 27th in a seven-furlong race at Beverley, a small North Country meeting. Carson worked hard to keep her in touch, and she finished sixth of the twenty-seven runners to a filly called Fragrant Rose. This reflected more to Carson's credit than to Bikini's.

Gamecourt raced over a mile at Newmarket on the 30th. As before, he watched the other horses and the starting gate and did not take much part in the race. Explaining his defeat to Jack Banks, who had again lost money on him, Carson said, 'He was never really interested. He was looking all over the place and just seemed to enjoy himself.'

Mountain Call atoned for these two by winning the Palace House Stakes at Newmarket on May 1st, giving weight all round. The start of this race was delayed when Dahban, the second favourite, took charge of his unfortunate jockey just as he was being pulled up at the starting stalls and bolted off across the Heath to the one-mile-five-furlong start. He was brought back at a trot and was about to rejoin the other horses when he took off again and galloped up the far side of the Sefton Course. He was withdrawn and did not come under Starter's Orders.

The race started three minutes late. Mountain Call took up the running at halfway and galloped on strongly to win by two lengths. Abbie West, who had beaten She Wolf at Newmarket two weeks earlier, finished far down the field. The race was over five furlongs in yielding going. Mountain Call won £2,372.

On May 9th Laureate ran at Chester, one of the oldest

courses in the country, where racing is recorded as early as
1540. It is a left-handed track, almost all of it on the bend. It
is therefore a very fast track, as whoever is on the rails cannot
afford to ease up at any point because he would lose his
position and would have to come again the longer way on the
outside.

Laureate's race was the ten-furlong Dee Stakes, for a first
prize of £1,938. He started the outsider of the field because of
his disgraceful performance at Thirsk. Carson's instructions
were, if no one else went on, to make the running himself. No
one else did go on, so he led all the way and won. Attalus, the
favourite, had tried to come to them inside the final furlong,
but Laureate would not be beaten.

Mountain Call, now established as Stanley House's star
three-year-old, mopped up the field in a relatively small race
at Kempton the next day. He carried top weight, and ran on
gamely to hold off a challenger in the final furlong.

Bikini ran with complete lack of distinction on the 13th,
finishing at the back of a big maiden field in an evening
meeting at Wolverhampton. Evening meetings are extras
put on during the summer and have no prestige in the racing
world. Bikini was strong enough, but Carson knew she had not
tried and thought her very backward. His opinion of her as a
slow, babyish filly was confirmed. He would have said so to
Ray Coppola when they were leading in, but the lad looked so
downcast that he kept the words back. It was the last race of
the evening, and darkness had fallen before Coppola got
Bikini loaded up for the journey home.

Meanwhile, Gamecourt was having his first overnight stay
away from home. He was entered at York in the Glasgow
Maiden Stakes on the 14th, and was to run in blinkers for the

first time. Jack Banks felt certain that this would do the trick. He meant to have a big bet on his colt, and had been saving up for it for some time.

Known as 'the Ascot of the North', York is a beautiful track, well laid out, and good to ride on. Its amenities – the layout of the Paddock in relation to the grandstand and the Tote; the easy availability of food and drink and other public commodities – are excellent, and the standard of racing is first-class.

After he exercised and settled his first lot on the 13th, Banks packed his bag for the night away from home. He bandaged Gamecourt's legs and put on knee boots to protect him during the journey. Just before they left, he changed Gamecourt's rug for a light sheet because it would be hot travelling in the horsebox.

They left at lunchtime with Michael Ryan in charge, and arrived at York at five o'clock. A high fence surrounded the racetrack stables, and they were stopped at the gate by a security guard. Banks handed in his identification, a stable lad's pass authorized by the Jockey Club, with his photograph and a physical description on it. He asked for the key to Gamecourt's box, which had been booked in advance. Gamecourt was unloaded and led into his box, which had been made up ready for him and had a bucket of fresh water in it. Banks took off the bandages and boots, straightened his colt up, and replaced the travelling sheet with a heavy rug. He took off Gamecourt's headcollar and went off to the canteen for a cup of tea, leaving the colt to relax.

He gave Gamecourt an hour or so to get used to his new loosebox, and used up the time by signing himself into the hostel and unpacking his overnight bag. The lads slept in

dormitories with about twenty beds to a room, each with a
storage locker beside it. Downstairs was a canteen and a place
where they could watch television. Back at the stables shortly
after six, Banks found Ryan giving Gamecourt a healthy feed
that he had brought up from Newmarket. Banks sprayed a
weak solution of Jeyes' Fluid all over Gamecourt's bed to
prevent him from eating it. It smelled unpleasant, but it was
only for one night and it was important that Gamecourt should
not over-eat before racing. After filling the haynet and refilling
the water bucket, Banks shut Gamecourt up for the night.

Ryan and Banks ate together in the canteen, where they
met lads from other stables whom they had not seen since the
summer before. Some of them decided to go and see a film,
others to drink in a local pub. Banks went to bed soon after
eleven, looking forward to the next day, confident that
Gamecourt had never looked better. He had brought a lot
of money with him from Newmarket to put on his colt, and
had stowed it safely in the locker beside his bed. Tomorrow
he would get a bet on; perhaps he would make a killing. Banks
drifted into sleep. In the stables, two security guards were
posted to keep watch over the horses.

In the morning the money was gone. Banks looked around
at the roomful of dressing lads, several of them friends of his,
and was depressed by the knowledge that one of them must
have taken it. How, he wondered, could someone in the same
position as himself rob him of the bet it had taken him so long
to save? He went out into the early morning and was slightly
comforted by Gamecourt, who was the kindest horse he had
ever had.

Michael Ryan got up at half past five and fed Gamecourt
with a bowl of corn at six. Banks mucked out the box and got

him ready for exercise. Other horses were already being led out to stretch their legs, the tougher ones clattering through the yard, mounted, for a pipe-opener on the racecourse. Banks slipped on Gamecourt's exercise bridle and led him out for a walk in the sun. The liver-chestnut coat shone and the muscles rippled under the velvety hide. Banks's depression began to lift, but he keenly regretted not being able to have a bet.

He brought Gamecourt back at nine o'clock and polished him over. There was no dust on the soft body-brush: Gamecourt's coat had been thoroughly clean before he had left for York. Ryan brought him another little feed, and the two lads went off for their own breakfast. Afterwards they came back to get the colt plated by the racecourse farrier. While Ryan plaited up Gamecourt's mane, Banks finished off his coat. At eleven o'clock they took away the water bucket and the haynet and put a muzzle on him in case he should be tempted by a bit of straw that Banks might have missed with the disinfectant. The muzzle, made of stiff leather with holes in it, covered Gamecourt's nose and mouth.

They left him like that, and went to get washed and changed and have a meal. With plenty of time in hand, they watched a couple of races on the hostel's television. Gamecourt would be running in the five o'clock, the last race on the card. It was over nine furlongs, a furlong longer than his last race, because van Cutsem felt he needed the extra distance. Two hours before the race Ryan and Banks went to get him ready. There had been a heavy shower at midday and the stable yard was wet.

They dressed him over and put on his racing bridle, which was made of fine, thin leather with straps only five-eighths of an inch wide. They put on Lord Derby's clean paddock rug and buckled it with a surcingle. When everything was ready, Banks stayed with his horse until it was time to lead him out.

Banks waited until other runners for the same race were being led out and then brought his colt out to follow them up to the racecourse. The presence of the other horses steadied Gamecourt, who was still green. The walk to the course, across a common dotted with people exercising dogs, took twenty minutes.

At the course they walked around in a small paddock, waiting while runners paraded for the four thirty. Bets were laid; then the crowd drifted away to watch the race and began to filter back. Bernard van Cutsem appeared with Michael Ryan, who carried one of Willie Carson's heavier saddles because Gamecourt, like all the colts in the race, had been allotted 126 pounds. Banks led him into a saddling stall, where van Cutsem took off the paddock rug and laid the number cloth neatly over Gamecourt's back. He then put on the weight cloth, already loaded with the extra lead that Carson would have to carry, then the saddle. He ran a surcingle round the lot for extra safety, holding it in position by running it through keepers on either side of the saddle. Then he put the paddock rug back on top. Ryan assisted him while Banks held the colt's head.

With Ryan at the head, Banks washed Gamecourt's legs to smarten them up, and arranged his quarters mark, a careful pattern of the hair on the hindquarters, just for show. He washed over Gamecourt's eyes and slipped a wet sponge into his mouth to comfort him in case it was dry. Van Cutsem fitted on the blinkers, which made Gamecourt tense up. It was time to go into the main paddock.

As Jack Banks walked Gamecourt round in front of the

curious crowd, he had never felt so confident. He could see on the Totalizator board that Gamecourt was fourth favourite. In the centre of the ring van Cutsem was talking to Carson and Ryan. Lord Derby had not been able to come this time.

The announcement for jockeys to mount was made. Banks turned Gamecourt in off the path so that he could not kick the paddock rails if he got upset. Gamecourt was jumpy, sweating a little from excitement. The Stanley House people joined them. Ryan took off the paddock rug and van Cutsem checked that the girths were tight. Then he gave Carson a leg up and Banks led them off on a final circuit of the paddock. He told Carson that he was on a winner this time. The jockey replied that he hoped the blinkers would do the trick; the colt certainly felt well. Banks took them out on to the course and let them go.

He hurried to the section of the stands reserved for stable lads and waited for his horse to come back. At first there was nothing to see; then a knot of flying horses who looked like ants in the distance. As they came nearer and Banks was able to distinguish them, he looked in vain among the leaders for a liver-chestnut face with a white star. Gamecourt came past the winning post eighth of the twenty-one runners. The black-jacketed Carson was riding hard with his hands and was using his whip, but it didn't do much good. Banks ran down to lead them in.

Gamecourt was sweaty, Carson tired and exasperated. 'He didn't do a bloody stroke,' he said. 'He's got the ability, but he won't try. The blinkers made him worse, if anything. *I* think he's very babyish.'

The disappointing baby was unsaddled, shampooed, and walked around to dry. He was a bit tucked up after his race, but perfectly well. He had an hour's rest in his racecourse loosebox. Banks came in with the bandages and knee boots, and got nuzzled in the back while he was putting them on. Gamecourt didn't seem at all ashamed of his performance.

They got back to Newmarket just before midnight. There was a warm mash waiting in the manger, packed in tightly with sacks over it to keep in the heat, since if it had been allowed to get cold it would have been sour and unpalatable. Gamecourt was glad to be home. He rolled in his own clean bed, drank a deep draught of water and snatched a mouthful of hay from his tightly stuffed haynet. Then he tucked into the mash. Parts of it were still too hot to eat, so he got his nose under them and threw them onto the floor to cool.

VIII

The final forfeit stage for the Derby and the Oaks fell on May 14th. Indolent was withdrawn because she had not yet raced as a three-year-old, She Wolf because of her damaged joint. The total forfeit paid for these two was £160.

Lord Derby's classic hopes for the season now rested with Laureate for the Derby and Laureate and She Wolf for the St Leger.

IX

Because of the good form he had shown at Chester and at Liverpool, Laureate was reasonably well fancied for the Derby Trial Stakes at Lingfield on May 17th. Lingfield is a pretty racecourse, midway between Brighton and London. The Derby Trial is its most important race of the season, and several of its winners have gone on to win the Derby. The track is sharp and tricky, with a steep descent to the final bend; an excellent test for a Derby entrant because Epsom has similar curves and gradients. A horse that cannot cope with Lingfield would have no chance in the Derby.

The going was yielding, which pleased Carson because he knew Laureate liked a bit of give in the ground. But he was up against some Derby probables, notably the good colt Torpid, who was favourite for the trial at 100–30. Laureate started joint third favourite at 5–1, linked in public opinion with a big, imposing-looking colt called Hurry Hurry.

Laureate looked the handsomest of the runners in the Paddock, behaving beautifully as Leaman led him round, with none of the messing about that he had shown before his bad Thirsk race. Since his Chester race had been won from in front, van Cutsem instructed Carson to keep him well up all the way.

Laureate jumped out of the stalls fast and settled into second place. The pace was not a great gallop, and with nine furlongs to go the field was closely bunched. Laureate took up the running at halfway and began to increase his lead. Carson appeared to be riding him out with his hands – almost pushing the horse along, swinging his arms forward with every stride. This made the other jockeys think that his mount had little left in reserve. In fact, Carson was quite unconscious of what he was doing; he was letting his hands go with the horse, and was not pushing him. His mounts were often reported to be 'pushed along' when they had not been. When he really meant to shake them up he would call out to them and click his tongue. Sometimes he would give them a backhander with the whip.

Laureate came away from the field fast. Seeing that he was still full of running, Torpid's jockey went after him, and these two raced well clear of the others. Torpid, under pressure, got near enough to challenge, but he faltered in the final furlong and Laureate, never really pressed, won comfortably by a length. The big Hurry Hurry, unable to cope with the sharp course, was third, six lengths away. His trainer immediately withdrew him from the Derby.

Carson was delighted. 'He held Torpid easily,' he told Lord Derby and van Cutsem. 'I knew he would win, but I gave him a little slap a hundred and fifty yards from the finish just to make certain. If he had been tackled in the straight he would still have found more.

'He's a funny horse. I think we're just starting to get to the bottom of him.'

Laureate's price shortened in the Derby betting. He went home a hero and was, on the following day, the object of general admiration when he was led out for exercise. Many of the Stanley House lads hurried to get their money on before his Derby price got even shorter. He was not to run again before the big race, so there was no chance that his form might be upset.

Stan Warren thought he was a wonderful horse. He had taken to calling him 'Twinkletoes'—a name that would not have occurred to anybody six months before—and visited him with a handful of grass on his evening rounds. Laureate would whinny out when he heard Warren's call. He was in splendid form, but there were eleven days still to go before the Derby. What could happen to stop him? Coughing. A knock at exercise. Someone might try to get at him if his odds got too short.

Meanwhile Mountain Call was taking things quietly. He had been entered for a race in France, but French governmental problems had stopped him from going over. It had been too late to enter him for a worthwhile race in England, so he had gained an unplanned holiday, and was enjoying it. He bucked and kicked going into the canters, but Arthur Bell, who was heavy for a stable lad, was able to hold him down.

Gamecourt was working extremely well. He led the canters in great spirits, looking the winner he had not proved himself to be. Maddock labelled him '... a morning glory. He likes working in the mornings, but not in the afternoons.' Warren did not think he would be anything out of the ordinary.

She Wolf had still not fully recovered from her damaged joint. She was sound enough to trot, but was not yet strong enough to be back in full work. It would be some time before she raced again, but her fine performance in the Nell Gwynn Stakes made her still a hopeful for the St Leger in September.

Bikini was, for the time being, the admiration of no one except Ray Coppola. She showed no sign of having learned anything from her three outings and seemed happy to go on being ignorant. Her trainer thought her useless, and Stan Warren agreed. Warren did not think very highly of Indolent, either. 'She may turn out well,' he said. 'She's a bit delicate on her feed. She may have more ability than Bikini.' Not much of a compliment. George Douglas was the only one who really thought her any good.

Surprisingly, he was quite right. Indolent had her first three-year-old race on May 24th in a maiden at Haydock over a mile. She cantered up, winning by two lengths. She was recorded as having been 'under pressure', but the reporter was fooled by Carson's style. She had finished nine lengths ahead of the favourite, Fragrant Rose, the filly who had won Bikini's Beverley race. Indolent certainly did have more ability than Bikini, and her stable thought more of her after that.

When the four-day declaration stage for the Derby came up on May 25th, the last £50 of entry fee was paid on Laureate's behalf. Of the initial 590 entries for the Derby, 282 had been scratched on November 21st, 203 on April 3rd, 70 on May 14th. At the four-day stage 22 more were taken out. Now there were thirteen horses left in.

The last days of May were sunny and showery. Tons of hay and straw were rolled down from the Stanley House lofts, and broken up and distributed into the big, shady looseboxes. Swallows' nests hung under the eaves. The horses led in from exercise and stayed for a while in the collecting paddock to pick the rich grass. Horseboxes were driven into the yard empty, and left with runners for late May meetings.

Monday, May 27th came: two days before the Derby, and the day before Laureate was to leave for Epsom. He looked magnificent as Tony Leaman rode him out to the Heath for Carson to give him his pipe-opener. He led him home, let him have a pick in the paddock, brought him in, rubbed him down, fed him, left him. In the late afternoon he came again and polished — it was quite unnecessary because Laureate's coat was sparkling clean — filled up his haynet, gave him clean water, fed him a specially delicious feed, and shut him up for the night. When Leaman had finished his own dinner, he came back with a handful of grass. The horse was sweet to him.

Laureate lay down to sleep. The night was clear and warm.

Stan Warren, making his evening rounds, called out, 'What are you doing, Twinkletoes?' Laureate whinnied back.

Tuesday, May 28th: Derby eve. Laureate had a lazy morning. Leaman took him out for an 'easy'; polished him again, fed him and left him. He went to pack up the things he would need for the big race.

Early in the afternoon the horsebox left for Epsom.

X

All over England people had put their money on for the Derby. Many planned to go to Epsom for the big race, many more to slip out of their offices and watch it on television.

Would Laureate be the one to win it for the first time for Lord Derby; be the horse who would finally fulfil his owner's ambition? It was also van Cutsem's ambition: he had not yet had a Derby winner either. He was afraid that Laureate might not have the finishing speed that a classic horse must have. But he had power and he would stay for ever.

Sir Ivor was still favourite, an apparently brilliant horse, but Stan Warren was not worried. He had faith in Laureate, and had backed him only to win.

In his bed in the Epsom hostel Tony Leaman tossed around in his sleep. He needed sleep, because he and his colt had a big day ahead. They had been together for six months. He remembered Laureate at the start – a mean face in the box that turned kind as the weeks went by; a horse that would whip round at exercise, and stop it if Leaman showed he did not mind; a horse that dropped him on the Severalls and spoiled the spring flowers. A victor at Liverpool, at Chester, at Lingfield.

XI

It might have been called the Bunbury, but for the toss of a coin. The 28-year-old twelfth Earl of Derby and his friend, Sir Charles Bunbury, were the men most responsible for founding the race. As the coin spun in the air, Derby made the right call; but Bunbury had his revenge – he entered the right horse. The first Derby was run in 1780, and Bunbury's colt, Diomed, won it.

The Derby originated as a mile-long race for three-year-old colts and fillies, modelled on the Oaks, which had been a great success on its first running in 1779. In 1784 the Derby distance was increased to a mile and a half, and so it has remained ever since. It is a race seldom won by a filly – out of a hundred and ninety-three runnings, only six fillies have been first past the post. The first filly to win it (Eleanor, 1801) also belonged to Sir Charles Bunbury.

In the late eighteenth century, and in the beginning of the nineteenth, racing was still largely the privilege of the rich. But by 1830, when the Derby had established itself as the most important race of the year, it had become the pleasure of the masses, and the business of many. Increasing newspaper publicity drew public attention, and the advent of the railway meant that horses and spectators no longer had to live within walking distance of Epsom. The Derby was a great event in mid-Victorian times. For most of the country it was a public holiday; even Parliament did not sit on Derby Day. Disraeli, in 1848, dubbed it 'the Blue Riband of the Turf'.

Scandals, frauds, and doping abounded in the nineteenth century. One of the coolest villains of the turf was Francis

Ignatius Coyle, who played a daring part in 1844, the year of the Great Swindle. The 1844 Derby was won by a horse entered as Running Rein, who was recognized by an Irish farmer as a four-year-old named Maccabaeus. An objection was lodged, and Running Rein's owner (presumably not part of the plot) brought an action for the recovery of the prize money. The all-important piece of evidence was the horse. A judge's order was issued for the training yard where it was stabled to be kept under close surveillance by detectives so that the horse could not be removed.

A day was quickly set for several veterinary surgeons to examine Running Rein to establish his age beyond doubt. Early on the morning of this critical day Ignatius Coyle, who had business with Running Rein's trainer, rode into the stable yard on his hack. When his business had been concluded, he remounted his hack and rode quietly away through the cordon of detectives.

The 'hack' he rode away on was Running Rein. The horse was never seen again.

The first foreign victory in the Derby was in 1865, by a French colt named Gladiateur who also won the Two Thousand Guineas and the St Leger. The French nicknamed him 'the Avenger of Waterloo'. The first American victory happened in 1881 with Iroquois, ridden by the great English jockey, Fred Archer. Archer won the Derby five times from 1877 to 1886. Late in 1886 he shot himself, having won every big race on the English Racing Calendar except for the Cesarewitch. He had been plagued by weight problems for much of his career (his winter weight was well over ten stone), and had wasted severely in the hope of winning the elusive Cesarewitch in the autumn of 1886. He lost the race by a nose.

If he had been one pound lighter he would have won. He was only twenty-nine when he died.

In 1897 the great American jockey Tod Sloan arrived in England. Until that time, English jockeys had raced with long stirrups, often using spurs, and races tended to be leisurely, with an accelerated pace over the last two furlongs. Sloan's style was different. Crouching low with short stirrups and short reins, getting off to a fast start and winning his races from in front, he was at first ridiculed by the English. But his style proved to be extremely effective. English jockeys soon learned to adapt to it, and have ridden short ever since. Although Sloan never won the Derby, compatriots of his who rode in the same manner won four of the first twelve Derbies of the twentieth century.

Derby surprises sometimes happen, but they are not common, because the form of the runners is usually so well known. A real surprise happened in 1908, when a filly called Signorinetta won at 100-1. Two days later she also won the Oaks. She never won another race, and was not notable at stud.

At the turn of the century, Derby luck ran with the Royal Family. The Prince of Wales won in 1896 with Persimmon, in 1900 with Diamond Jubilee, and, as King Edward VII, with Minoru in 1909. His son, George V, would have had a good chance with Anmer in 1913, but for the most bizarre event in the history of the Derby: a suffragette named Emily Davidson threw herself in front of Anmer as the field came round Tattenham Corner. She succeeded in bringing the horse down, and died later of her injuries. Anmer recovered.

During the First World War the army requisitioned Epsom and the race was moved to Newmarket. Steve Donoghue, who rode the winner six times between 1915 and 1925, was so much in demand as a jockey that he commanded a fee of £7,000 to ride in the Derby. In 1918 Lady James Douglas became the first woman to own a Derby winner (Gainsborough).

Between 1922 and 1941 Fred Darling trained the winner seven times. The thirties were dominated by the Aga Khan, who spent an enormous amount of money on racing, and was repaid with five Derby winners: Blenheim in 1930, Bahram in 1935, Mahmoud (who set up the record time of 2 minutes 33.8 seconds, which still stands) in 1936, My Love in 1948, and Tulyar in 1952.

1933 was Hyperion's year. His owner, the seventeenth Earl of Derby (Lord Derby's grandfather), had won the Derby before, in 1924, with Sansovino, and again in 1942 with Watling Street. The war years were splendid years for him: Watling Street was also second in the Two Thousand Guineas and the St Leger; Herringbone won the 1943 One Thousand Guineas and St Leger; Garden Path won the Two Thousand Guineas in 1944. In 1945 his Sun Stream won both the One Thousand Guineas and the Oaks.

The 1938 Derby was a bit of freakish good luck. It was won by Bois Roussel, owned by Peter Beatty. As late as six weeks before the race Beatty had been looking for a Derby runner, none of his own being good enough. His trainer, the great Fred Darling, persuaded him to accompany him to France, where they saw Bois Roussel win a good race at Longchamp on April 10th. Beatty bought him for £8,000. His Derby winnings a few weeks later were £42,000. 1938 was also the first time the race was shown on television.

During the war the Derby was again moved to Newmarket.

It returned to Epsom immediately after the war, but the 1946 race was disappointing. The French trainers had not thought the war would end when it did, so no French contestants had been nominated at the preliminary stage of entry. It was not a great field, and Airborne won, in the slowest time for twenty years – 2 minutes 44.8 seconds.

The French more than made up for missing the 1946 Derby. Between 1948 and 1965 they took the famous English prize six times. The Irish, too, were a great threat to English-trained horses, winning in 1958, 1962, and 1964.

In 1954 the Derby was won by the American-bred Never Say Die, ridden by Lester Piggott. Piggott was only eighteen, the youngest Derby-winning jockey of the century, and possibly the youngest of all time (the age of the boy who won on Caractacus in 1862 is not known). Piggott won again in 1957 on Crepello, and in 1960 on St Paddy. In St Paddy's race the French-trained favourite, Angers, broke a leg after six furlongs and had to be destroyed.

In 1962, seven horses fell in the worst pile-up in the history of the race. The winner that year was Larkspur, owned by Mr Raymond Guest, the American Ambassador to Ireland, and trained in Ireland by the brilliant Vincent O'Brien.

In recent years, as the form of Derby entrants gets more and more widely published, the winner of the race is frequently the favourite. Derby favourites won in 1964, 1965, and 1967. Lester Piggott, Champion Jockey in England since 1964 and one of the finest judges of a racehorse in the world, turned freelance in 1967 and so could ride his choice of the Derby entrants. In 1968, the 189th running of the Derby Stakes, the favourite was the Two Thousand Guineas winner Sir Ivor, American-bred and owned by Raymond Guest;

trained in Ireland by Vincent O'Brien; ridden by Piggott, the champion.

XII

The Epsom mile and a half is considered to be the greatest all-round test of a three-year-old in the world. A Derby horse must have both speed and stamina, and must be able to gallop both on rising and on falling ground and handle sharp, left-handed corners and a right-handed curve. It is a hard course for the jockey, too. (Asked by an amateur jockey for advice on how to ride at Epsom, Lester Piggott is reported to have answered, 'Don't do that. You'd end up in the tea tent.')

The Derby start is on the flat at the far side of the course. The runners jump off and sweep right-handed uphill to a gradual left-hander, seven furlongs from home. They run left-handed down the hill to the famous sharp left turn of Tattenham Corner. Turning into the straight they bounce on to a road and off it again, run down a hill into a dip and gallop the last furlong on an uphill rise. It is the supreme test of the thoroughbred, and the moment the winner passes the post its stud value is assured at upwards of £250,000.

There are no conditions attached to entries. Any three-year-old colt or filly may run if its owner is willing to pay the entry fee, which in 1968 amounted to £200. The prizes that year were £58,525.50 and a £500 gold trophy to the winner, £17,330 to the second, £8,565 to the third, and £2,429.50 to the fourth.

On the morning of Wednesday May 29th, Willie Carson walked the course. It was to be his first Derby ride, and he needed to know every inch of Epsom. He had been very excited the night before and had trouble getting to sleep. Since the race at Thirsk he had been riding Laureate nearly every time he worked, and he thought he had an excellent chance.

It was a sweltering hot day. As he walked, Carson passed people who had slept the night at Tattenham Corner to establish good vantage points for themselves. When he finally reached the winning post his shirt was sticking to his back and he longed to buy an ice-cream from one of the stalls in the fairground. The area opposite the grandstands had filled up overnight. Fortune-tellers, many of them gipsies in costume, sat at the entrances to brightly-coloured booths; pearly kings and queens jostled in the crowd, a full-sized fair was in operation. Bookies were already chalking up the prices on their boards, and tipsters were everywhere. On the stands side of the course, which was more dignified, people in smart summer dresses and suits began to appear. Here and there a top hat and tails could be seen, though these were mostly in the Royal Box. Some had booked lunch in the clubhouses, others brought picnic baskets and champagne and ate beside the track. By two o'clock, when the first race started, there were 30,000 people on the course.

After the second race there was an hour to wait until the Derby, taken up by an extra-long period in the Paddock and by a parade of the runners before the stands. The owners drank champagne and tried to look calm. In the weighing room all of the jockeys, no matter how experienced, were nervous (they would be all right once they were up). The trainers worked off some of the tension with last-minute orders and organization. The stable lads and travelling head lads made tiny adjustments to their horses' clothing and tried not to communicate their excitement. But the horses all felt it.

It was time to go into the Paddock. The Queen and the Royal party had already walked down from the Royal Box and were waiting in the middle of a circle of perfect green. At the foot of the stands another perfect green circle, much smaller, waited for the winner to come back.

The Paddock was dominated by Sir Ivor, a big, handsome bay colt who had been unbeaten in his last five races, most important in the Two Thousand Guineas. There were still some doubts about whether he could stay the distance, since neither his sire nor his dam had won races longer than a mile and a furlong, but Piggott was reported to have called him a racing certainty.

There were thirteen runners. Others who looked impressive were Connaught, a bay colt with a white face who had been hopelessly outdistanced by Sir Ivor in the Two Thousand Guineas but whose performance a week later in the Chester Vase had shown a vast improvement; Remand, a chestnut colt by Alcide, who had beaten Connaught half a length in the Chester Vase; Mount Athos, a bay who had won both his three-year-old races comfortably; and Torpid, whom Laureate had beaten at Lingfield. There were no fillies, no French entries, and only two Irish-trained runners. The outsider of the field was a colt called First Rate Pirate, who belonged to a pop singer. He had done absolutely nothing, had no chance whatsoever, and was only there for the fun of the thing. Bookies were offering him at 500–1.

Laureate himself looked as handsome as any. He was turned out to perfection, and was following Leaman quietly round the ring. He was fancied at 100–8, and was fourth favourite.

Sir Ivor was well established at 5–4 on, Remand stood at 4–1 and Connaught at 100–9. The betting was 25–1 bar these four.

The jockeys came into the Paddock. Carson, in the white cap and black silk jacket with the famous white button of Lord Derby's first colours, went over to join Derby and van Cutsem, both of whom were wearing morning dress. The horses were turned into the centre of the ring, the jockeys got up, and the lads led them out for the Parade.

The Parade was itself a test for a horse. The runners were led before the stands in the order in which they had been drawn. Thousands of people watched them, and the noise and tension of the crowd was quite enough to upset a nervous horse. Several of them sweated up. Derbys have been lost in the past at this point because horses got over-excited.

They turned and cantered away to the starting stalls. Laureate moved beautifully, flicking his forelegs out in a way that showed he could quickly lengthen his stride if asked. Sir Ivor ate up the ground with a long, deep stride. Piggott pulled him back to a trot, and they came down to the post last.

They walked around behind the starting gate. Laureate had gone down to the start coolly enough. He had been very cool in the Paddock, but now he began to break out into a sweat. Carson, who had never before seen him show the slightest concern about racing, put it down to the extra tension of Derby Day. When the runners were loaded into the stalls, Laureate appeared to be very calm. Carson had him gathered together not quite up to the barrier in front, perhaps meaning to get him moving a second before the gates opened and so be fast away. Laureate had been drawn number five, in the centre of the field, which would mean he would have to get in front at the start if he were not to be cut off by the right-hand curve.

The Starter's hand came down and the gates in front flew open. Laureate jumped out with the leaders and ran with them for the first furlong. Carson took a pull at him. Benroy, an outsider, settled down in the lead, followed by Connaught, Society, and Laureate. The pace was reasonably slow. They swept right-handed up the hill, passed the mile gate, and turned across the course into the left-hand bend at the top of the hill. Laureate moved up into third place. The pace got faster.

Halfway down the hill to Tattenham Corner, Benroy began to weaken and dropped out. Connaught took it up, with Laureate lying second on his outside by a neck to half a length. Sir Ivor was some way behind in the middle of the field, just ahead of Remand. At the back of the field Mount Athos began to improve. First Rate Pirate was tailed off a long way last.

At Tattenham Corner it was Connaught from Laureate, Society, Atopolis, Remand, and Sir Ivor. The field was fairly tightly bunched and Laureate was going so well that Carson had to sit against him to stop him from taking the lead too soon. They turned into the straight with three furlongs to go. The noise of the crowd became a roar.

And then he stopped, or so it seemed to Carson. He had been tearing along in a very good position when they came into the straight. In a few yards he dropped his bit and shortened his stride. All of the field except Benroy and First Rate Pirate, the two back markers, went past him very quickly. Carson seemed to be riding a different horse. Ahead, Connaught kept his lead and looked to have the race in hand, but Sir Ivor produced a terrific burst of speed, almost as though he had an extra gear, and swept into the lead less than a hundred yards from the post. He won by 1½ lengths from Connaught and Mount Athos. Remand was fourth.

Laureate tailed in eleventh, a long way back. He was a very tired horse. Tony Leaman came up and took his bridle. He could find nothing to say. Carson was bitterly disappointed, but Lord Derby, who must have felt just as unhappy, smiled at him and said, 'Never mind.' Bernard van Cutsem took it best because he had not really expected anything.

No one said much.

EPILOGUE

Epilogue

THERE was no immediate explanation for Laureate's distressing Derby performance. 'If he had shown his form, he should have finished in the first three,' van Cutsem said. 'But he chucked it.' It had been a hard race for the colt, and he was rested from racing for the next six weeks. But his work at home in June 1968 was just as it had always been. He looked well. Tony Leaman and Willie Carson said he felt well.

Bernard van Cutsem entered him next for the Princess of Wales's Stakes, run over a mile and a half at Newmarket on July 9th, with a first prize of £2,469. There was a high-class field, including Mount Athos, the Derby third, and Attalus, close second to Laureate at Chester and now meeting him on better terms by eight pounds.

Laureate's good races at Chester and Lingfield had been won from in front, and Carson had instructions to make the running at Newmarket. Accordingly, he jumped his colt out fast and pushed him into the lead. Laureate, normally a hard puller, did not seem too keen. 'He was never on the bit,' Carson said afterwards. 'I kept hoping he'd go, but he didn't. We came into the straight second on sufferance. I was riding him out with my hands. Three and a half furlongs out we dropped back fast. When we were last, I gave him a crack with the whip. He didn't respond.' Mount Athos went on to win by two lengths from Attalus. Laureate finished last.

Obviously there was something wrong. Laureate was taken

home and examined by the veterinary surgeon. A cardiograph showed he had a weak heart.

He did not race again. He had won over £5,000 in prize money and was beautifully bred, so Lord Derby decided to sell him for stud. He came up for auction at Tattersalls's December Sales at Newmarket on December 4th. He was stubborn about entering the sale ring, stuck his toes in and would not go, trying to spin round. Once they had him in the ring he behaved perfectly. The auctioneer proposed an opening bid of 6,000 guineas for him. It was immediately taken up, and bidding rose quickly to 22,000 guineas. He was eventually bought by the Keith Freeman Bloodstock Agency, on behalf of a syndicate of South African breeders. He began his life as a stallion at the Knoffelfontein Stud in Cape Province, South Africa.

Van Cutsem thought Laureate would make a fine stallion. 'He was a very elegant horse,' he said. 'I liked him very much.'

II

It promised to be a good summer for Mountain Call. He began it 'widely acclaimed as the fastest sprinter in the country' (*Sporting Life*), but in the Temple Stakes at Sandown on June 4th he was beaten a neck by D'Urberville, who had beaten him at level weights at Doncaster the September before.

It was Russ Maddock's last ride on him. Mountain Call's next race was at Royal Ascot on June 20th, while Maddock was away in France riding another of van Cutsem's horses. In his absence the ride was offered to Lester Piggott, and thereafter it was Piggott who rode Mountain Call in all his races.

It was no disgrace to Maddock to be 'jocked off' in favour

of Piggott. Owners and trainers often change jockeys, feeling perhaps that another man will get on better with their horse. If a horse has been losing regularly this is understandable, but not infrequently a change will be made when the outgoing jockey has done extremely well with the horse. As, indeed, Maddock had with Mountain Call. But that kind of thinking did not apply to the case of Mountain Call. Maddock was, and remained, first jockey to van Cutsem, and the partnership continued to do extremely well.

Before racing Mountain Call, Piggott rode work on him on the Heath. Mountain Call's practice of bucking as he went into a gallop still held. Arthur Bell, who was a heavy lad, could usually stay on him, but lightweights who did not know his ways would almost always come unstuck. On the morning of Piggott's first ride on Mountain Call the colt excelled himself: going into the gallops he did a particularly big buck which sent the champion flying. Mountain Call ran off towards the Bury Road, looking for a victim, and found Ted Leader's hack. The riderless colt reared up and grabbed hold of its neck with his teeth. Leader fought him off, lashing out desperately with his whip. Stan Warren galloped up on his pony and managed, just in time, to get Mountain Call to go back to work.

Mountain Call and Piggott won the Cork and Orrery Stakes at Royal Ascot and the Prix Maurice de Gheest at Deauville on August 1st. They were second in the July Cup at Newmarket, beaten four lengths by the good sprinter So Blessed at level weights, but here Mountain Call had his revenge on D'Urberville who, also carrying the same weight, could only manage fifth place, and on Be Friendly, who had just beaten him in the Vernons' November Sprint Cup the year before. Van Cutsem summed him up as 'a charming horse to deal with'.

Mountain Call had been racing hard since April, so after his victory at Deauville he was given a rest. He did not race again for seven weeks, when he had a warm-up in the Avington Stakes at Kempton on September 20th. He won in what the *Sporting Life* described as 'a nice exercise gallop'. In the Diadem Stakes at Ascot a week later (the 28th) he was unaccountably badly beaten into third place. It seemed a repeat of his week at Deauville the year before, but there had been no sea air to excuse it.

On October 18th he beat a field of high-class sprinters at Newmarket in the Challenge Stakes, turning the tables on Great Bear, who had finished just in front of him in the Diadem. His breeder, Dr John Burkhardt, was there to see the race. 'I feel very proud of him,' he said. 'He's one of those extraordinary horses who does just what he has to just when he is required to.' He attributed the colt's success to everyone who had handled him from birth on, and especially to Arthur Bell, whose relationship with the horse had struck him as outstandingly good.

Mountain Call's last race of the season was to be the Vernons' November Sprint Cup on November 9th, the last day of the flat. The entries included Be Friendly and So Blessed, and the racing fraternity anticipated a thrilling match, but on the day of the race fog covered the course at Haydock and racing was abandoned.

Mountain Call had won more than £18,000 and had established himself as one of the best sprinters in the country. Most owners would have been tempted to retire him to stud at the end of his three-year-old season, especially since many sprinters seem to lose their form as four-year-olds, but Isaac Kornberg sportingly decided to keep him on in training. Early in 1969 he sold a half-share in him to Lord Derby.

At four years old, Mountain Call was not as brilliant as he had been at two or three. His winnings for the season came to only £3,631.6. It may have been that his interest in racing waned as he got older, or perhaps he was simply up against a better class of horse – the three-year-old sprinters of 1969 were exceptional. In his first race as a four-year-old, the Abernant Stakes at Newmarket on April 17th, he was beaten three lengths by the aptly-named three-year-old Song (by Sing Sing out of Intent), who subsequently turned out to be the most brilliant sprinter in the country. He had become more coltish and comparatively (for him) obstreperous in the box. His laziness at home was more pronounced than ever, and it was only with the greatest difficulty that he could be persuaded to overtake his regular work companion, an eight-year-old selling plater. *

He began to assert his masculinity in the Paddock at race meetings. He would kick out at the Paddock rails, or at the sides of the stall where he was being saddled. Sometimes, if he thought the saddling enclosure offered too many targets, van Cutsem would saddle him off the course. Mountain Call was getting a reputation for idleness on the track, and Piggott had to use all of his brilliance to get the best out of him. He was second in the Prix du Palais Royal at Longchamp on May 18th, and fourth (the only time in over two years that he had finished out of the first three) on June 19th at Royal Ascot in the Cork and Orrery, which he had won the year before.

* A selling plate is a race in which all the runners may be claimed for small prices, and the winner must be offered for auction with a low reserve. Thus a 'selling plater' is usually a horse of little value.

But Mountain Call was not through. He came back with a bang in the Portland Handicap at Doncaster on September 11th – a brilliant bit of timing by van Cutsem, who had saved him up all summer for this important race – and lamed himself in the Paddock before the race by kicking the Paddock rails. He was examined and was considered sound enough to start. He beat a good field in style, though Piggott was hard put to it to make him do it, and once more won praise from the press ('Mountain Call is not only a very fast horse, at home on all types of ground and equally effective over five and six furlongs, but he is a handsome and powerful individual who should have a fine career at stud' – *The Times*). He had his last race at Maisons-Laffitte on September 22nd, beaten a short head and two lengths in the Prix de Seine et Oise.

In October 1969 Mountain Call retired to stud. In his three years of racing he had won £22,439.55. He now stands at Woodlands, Newmarket, where Alcide stood before him. His fee is 600 guineas a mare.

Mountain Call's life as a stallion began appallingly: nothing could induce him to cover a mare. He was sent for therapy to Bolton Stud, Yorkshire, where he had spent some months as a foal with his dam, Cloudy Walk. Whatever was done to him at Bolton worked like a charm. He returned to Woodlands, and of the forty-two mares he covered in his first season, thirty-eight produced foals. Most, like himself, were chestnut, smallish, and compact.

III

Gamecourt ran at Epsom in a ten-furlong race for three-year-olds the day after the Derby. Jack Banks had suggested to van Cutsem that, because he led so well at home, the answer might be to front-run him. Carson had orders to keep him on the outside, away from the press of horses which it could be assumed he did not much like, and to keep him up with the leaders. Gamecourt, who wore blinkers, jumped out but would not go: the Form Book said he 'dwelt'. He made some headway three furlongs out and finished halfway down the field. He was never nearer.

After that, van Cutsem took the blinkers off him because they seemed to make him, if anything, worse. Gamecourt's work at home proved that he had ability, and there was no alternative but to force him to show it on a racecourse. On August 5th he ran at Folkestone in a maiden race over the Derby distance. Carson rode with long stirrups and used spurs. The long stirrups allowed him to get the spurs into his mount.

Folkestone is a right-handed track. Gamecourt ran round the middle of it, hanging badly to the left. Horses who hang to one side do so either because there is something wrong with them or because they are trying to get out of racing. Carson was quite sure that Gamecourt was trying to get out of it. At one point he hung so badly that Carson had to hit him on the side of the head to get him to turn into the straight. He made all the running and won by seven lengths, and won pulling up. Had he run round the inside of the track his time would have been phenomenal. As it was, Gamecourt's time of 2 minutes 33.3 seconds over twelve furlongs is a track record at Folkestone that stands today.

He ran again at Pontefract on August 16th in a four-horse field that included two other winners. Again Carson wore spurs, and Gamecourt made all the running and won by a length. On September 26th at Beverley, in a mixed-age race, he carried top weight on the weight-for-age scale, and was one of only two three-year-olds in the race. He led for much of the way and finished fifth, having shown fair form against some proven older horses. Jack Banks said that he had not looked well before the race.

It was difficult to know what to do with Gamecourt. Van Cutsem thought him only a fair horse – good enough in bad company always to be in front. Despite his improved performances on the racecourse he had not beaten anything special, was not naturally competitive, and had shown quite clearly that he did not like racing. What he did appear to enjoy was galloping about on his home ground. He very rarely worked badly at home, and was an excellent lead horse. Van Cutsem's former lead horse, Quadruple, was about to be retired, so he asked Lord Derby if he could keep Gamecourt on as the new lead horse.

It made Banks glad. He was devoted to Gamecourt. 'He was the kindest horse I ever had,' he said. 'He had no vices whatsoever and was very affectionate. When I took him his food he used to call out to me.'

So Gamecourt stayed in training through the winter of 1968–9. There was always concern about his condition: he was a narrow, fragile-looking horse whose hindquarters never really rounded out. Even when he had been racing, his coat had never taken on the really glossy, velvety sheen that most thoroughbreds have. In the coldest parts of winter he had always needed an infra-red light in his box.

Early in the spring of 1969 he led the gallops on the Heath two or three times a week, occasionally galloping with both lots. He was often used to try out other horses. He would set a good gallop and let himself be overtaken in the last furlong.

Banks felt sure that he would become bored with it, but, as he had the summer before, he worked so well that once again van Cutsem was tempted to race him.

Gamecourt ran his last race on March 25th. It was a small race at Doncaster over ten furlongs. Soon after the start he got bumped by one of the other runners and was squeezed into the rails. The experience upset him, and Carson could get no further effort out of him. He finished twelfth.

He had run badly, despite the obvious excuse. It seemed probable that there was something physically wrong with him. When he got home, the veterinary surgeon was sent for. His diagnosis was kidney trouble, which is incurable. Gamecourt was destroyed.

IV

The bad joint that had kept She Wolf off the racetrack throughout May grew strong again, and by the end of the month she was back in work. She still made a noise after doing fast work, which was worrying for van Cutsem and Lord Derby. Derby planned, eventually, to keep her on as a brood mare. Physically she was a lovely filly. She had been second in both her races so far, putting up excellent performances in good company. Though it was by then too late to hope to pick up a classic race with her, it would greatly add to her value at stud if she could be made to win a race of any kind.

She ran in a ten-and-a-half furlong race at York on June 15th. It was not an important race and, although two of the other entries were already winners, She Wolf so far outclassed the rest of the field in appearance and on form that she was made favourite at 5–2 on. This meant that in the opinion of the crowd she was virtually certain to win. She came into the straight in touch with the leaders, nicely placed for a final burst, but more than a furlong from home she staggered. It seemed to Carson that she had run out of breath, and he stopped pressing her because he was sure that there was something seriously wrong. She finished last. As before, she pulled up making a nasty noise.

There were speculations afterwards that she might have swallowed her tongue. Horses will sometimes do this, obstructing the windpipe and half choking themselves. In the time taken to pull the horse up and get someone to look in its mouth, the horse has often managed to get its tongue back into the normal position. Or her behaviour could have been caused by a 'soft palate'; paralysis of the soft palate, which lies between the nasal passages and the larynx and is partly responsible for the separation of the windpipe from the gullet, can cause the noise that is associated with swallowing the tongue. Alternatively, She Wolf could have 'gone in the wind', a phrase meaning that there is an obstruction to the air flow somewhere between the nasal passages and the lungs. This could be due to a tumour or other kind of lump, or it could be caused by temporary paralysis of the vocal cords. The larynx – the entrance to the windpipe and also the floor of the throat – controls the proper direction of food and air. The opening into it can be enlarged or reduced by the movement of the vocal cords. If these become paralysed the flow of air into the windpipe will be obstructed. This paralysis can be cured by 'Hobdaying': an operation to immobilize the vocal cords, pioneered by Professor Hobday.

In a case where there is an obstruction in the wind, the noise made by the sufferer will be loudest at a gallop. The greater the airflow, the greater the effect. Since the muscles governing the airflow are under nervous control, interference can be caused by nervous spasm and a horse who makes a noise need not necessarily have anything physically wrong with it.

A horse has an extremely long breathing apparatus. It is possible to look up his nose as far as the larynx, but impossible to see into the windpipe or the lungs. X-rays are impracticable because the horse will not keep still. After a thorough examination the veterinary surgeon could find nothing the matter with She Wolf. Subsequently Maureen Foley reported that the filly felt perfectly normal at exercise.

She Wolf had always made a noise at work or when racing, but it had not previously seemed to be associated with any physical distress. It seemed reasonable, therefore, to assume that during her York race she had swallowed her tongue. Bernard van Cutsem decided to race her in a tongue strap, which would prevent her from doing this. He entered her in an evening meeting at Teesside Park on July 8th. The public had apparently ascribed her bad York performance to an off-day, because she was again made favourite. She jumped off in front and led until two furlongs out. Then she weakened fast, and gave Carson the same kind of feel that she had given him at York. Once more she blew disastrously, and once again a physical cause could not be found. During the race she had managed, despite the tongue strap, to get her tongue loose.

She left Stanley House Stables two days later. There was no point in keeping her in training. If she had, in fact, gone in the wind it would make no difference to her as a brood mare. She was turned out at Woodlands, a new member of the Stanley House Stud. In the spring of 1969 she was sent to Lavington to visit Relko.

V

Bikini never learned to race. If her first three races had been undistinguished, her last was worse. She ran in a minor handicap at Beverley on June 13th and was never in the race. She finished seventh of the eight runners.

At three-and-a-half years old, Bikini's only contribution to racing had been to teach Ray Coppola to understand racehorses. She had been friendly, amiable, and tractable from birth. 'She never put a foot wrong all the way through,' Stan Warren said. 'She never threw anyone off. She was really too quiet. Probably that was why she was no good as a racehorse.' Even Coppola said she had been 'a little bit *too* soft'.

Keeping her in training was a waste of money. She was sent up to Tattersalls's July Sales, where she was sold for 5,400 guineas (just about enough to cover Lord Derby's outlay on her). She went to stud in New Zealand. Mick Ryan said she would make a marvellous brood mare.

VI

'Indolent turned out very useful at the back end of her three-year-old season,' Stan Warren said. So she did. The ugly duckling with the plain head and the workmanlike body who had surprised her stable by cantering up in the Willows Maiden Plate on May 24th ran next in the Lancashire Oaks at Haydock on June 8th. This, a mile-and-a-half race worth £1,253.40 to the winner, was won by a very good filly called Bringley, who beat Indolent into second place by six lengths. This form was not quite fair to Indolent, who had hung to the

right during the race. Two days later she was found to be
lame in her near fore. For the next two weeks she was too
unsound to go out for exercise, and stayed in her box with a
muscle vibrator on her leg. She lost, of course, a lot of condition because of her inactivity, and it was not until August
that van Cutsem thought her fit to race again.

She was entered for the Darley Brewery Handicap, a £1,830
race at Pontefract on August 26th. She had a warm-up in a
minor race, the Cobholm Plate at Yarmouth on the 21st, which
she won very easily. In the Pontefract race, for which she
started favourite under the joint-top weight of 126 pounds,
she had an unlucky run. Willie Carson said, 'She got into a lot
of trouble from the other horses. There was a big field and we
couldn't get by. We were on the inside, and there were horses
in front of us and to the side. They were bunched around us. I
had to snatch Indolent up.' Indolent slipped and went down
on her knees. She was struck into from behind by one of the
other runners, but she managed to get back on her feet.
Turning into the straight there were only four horses behind
her of the thirteen runners. Carson got her clear. She passed
half the field in the remaining two-and-a-half furlongs and
was running on strongly at the finish, but even so she was only
placed fifth.

On September 5th she ran again at Haydock in a small race
for three- and four-year-olds, the Hermitage Green Stakes.
She started favourite at the ridiculous odds of 7–1 on, her
nearest rival in the betting being 10–1. There were only two
other runners, neither with any form. 'She won in an absolute
canter, an exercise canter,' Carson said. 'She made the running at half speed, having a good look round with her ears
pricked. She wasn't even blowing when she pulled up.'

Then she ran in the Sun Chariot Stakes, an important race at Newmarket on October 5th, finishing fifth in a high-class field and weakening towards the end. Carson felt that her performance was no disgrace.

Van Cutsem thought her worth sending to France for the bigger French prizes, and entered her for the Prix des Aigles at Longchamp on October 13th. George Douglas took her over two days before the race – she travelled excellently by air. Willie Carson went over, too, and stayed the night. It was the first time he had ever been to France. On the morning of the race he walked the course, and later in the day he rode Indolent to win by two lengths. As they came into the Winners' Enclosure, George Douglas leading, the crowd cheered Carson and slapped him on the back as if he had won the Derby. 'What would they have done if you'd lost?' Douglas asked him.

Indolent came back to England and then returned to France on October 28th for the Prix de Flore, a £10,000 race at Saint-Cloud. 'The ground was sloshy-heavy,' Carson said, 'but Indolent didn't mind too much. We finished fourth. We were quite pleased with her. She was a game filly.'

The flat season had finished again. Bernard van Cutsem liked Indolent; he didn't think she was a first-class performer, but he rated her top second-class. He wanted to keep her in training and tried to persuade Lord Derby to his point of view, but the Stanley House Stud needed brood mares and Derby felt he must retire her.

So Indolent joined Lord Derby's stud. She was turned out at Woodlands and grew the rough winter coat of a brood mare. In 1970 she had a bay filly foal by Stupendous. It looked a lot like her.

VII

The horses, and some of the people, have changed at New-market since this book was begun, but the spirit of the great training grounds will always be the same. On the Heath, on any morning, upwards of two thousand horses exercise in elegant strings. Each carries the hopes of a stable lad, an owner, a jockey, or a trainer.

Tragedy has come to some. Mick Ryan died of a heart attack in April 1972. At Woodlands, where he served so well, the stud groom is now Jack Relihan.

Russ Maddock will probably never race again. In October 1969, his right leg was badly broken in a three-horse pile-up in a maiden stakes at Newbury. More than a year went by before he was fit enough to ride; then, with great courage and perseverance – at fifty, broken bones do not heal easily – Maddock got back into the saddle. By March 1971 he was strong enough to ride work. Then, just before the racing season started, a filly dropped him on the gallops. She lashed out with her hind feet, catching Maddock in the worst possible place – she shattered his slowly-mending right knee.

In October 1970 Colonel Adrian Scrope retired from Woodlands to become director of Lord Howard de Walden's blood-stock interests. Lord Derby's new stud manager is Dr John Burkhardt. He is glad to be in charge of Mountain Call again, and is delighted with the stallion's first crop of foals, who are now selling well as yearlings.

Doug Smith, Lord Derby's former first jockey, has done extremely well in the short time he has been training. Part of his success must be due to his excellent head lad: Stan Warren.

Smith was fifth in the list of leading trainers in 1971. This year, his string of two-year-olds includes a nice-looking filly belonging to the Earl of Derby. She is called Wolverene, and is by Relko out of She Wolf. Like her dam, she ran for the first time on September 8th in the good-class Devonshire Maiden Stakes at Doncaster. Ridden by Willie Carson, she finished sixth of the fourteen runners. The Form Book said she had been for the most part behind in the race, but had run on well at the end to finish only seven lengths behind the winner.

Willie Carson, the late starter, has turned out brilliantly and, barring accidents, will become the Champion Jockey of 1972. He continues to ride Lord Derby's horses, and is also first jockey to Bernard van Cutsem, who is currently fourth in the list of leading trainers. One of the two-year-olds Carson rides for van Cutsem is Miss Winkle, Indolent's first foal. A big workmanlike filly with a plain head, she is expected to make a good three-year-old.

Of Bikini, carrying on Hyperion's line on the other side of the world, there is no news; but Laureate, a successful stallion in South Africa, is highly thought of. His stud manager, D. W. Silcock, reports that he is 'very proud, very quick-thinking. Sometimes he plays like a youngster, and he is hard to keep in a respectable condition because he gets fat very easily. He is easy to work with, and tame; he gets annoyed if hit, but is never savage. He is a lovable, masculine horse, and his stock are pleasing and good-natured.'

She Wolf and Indolent, both members of the Stanley House Stud, are summering at Knowsley with their foals. She Wolf has a very nice chestnut filly by Silly Season, and Indolent a handsome chestnut colt by Royal Palace, the 1967 Derby winner. Colin Dive says it is almost time to wean them.